Thorpe

The Lost Autobiography of an American Icon

By

Anita Thorpe

Dedication

To the enduring legacy of Jim Thorpe, a champion on and off the field. This book is dedicated to his family, friends, and the countless fans who tirelessly championed his name and fought for justice. A special thanks to Robert "Bob" Wheeler and Florence Ridlon, whose unwavering dedication and a serendipitous discovery in the Library of Congress unlocked the truth and paved the way for the restoration of Jim's rightful place in Olympic history. And finally, to the Bright Path Strong organization and the 75,000 signatories who added their voices to the chorus, and to my father, Richard, and his siblings, whose lifelong passion ensured Jim Thorpe's legacy would never be forgotten.

To the Library of Congress, guardian of American culture. For their unwavering commitment to collecting and preserving our nation's literary heritage, and for twice playing a critical role in safeguarding the invaluable information surrounding the American icon Jim Thorpe, we offer our deepest appreciation. Hail to our forefathers, who, in their wisdom, forged this rich and accessible resource for every citizen.

Acknowledgment

I'd like to express my deepest gratitude to the late *Orlo Robertson* and his family. Without his profound love of sports and a good story, this book would simply not exist.

I would like to extend my sincere gratitude to *Dr. Barbara Bair*, *Manuscript Division* and the *Library of Congress* for providing access to the historical letters and personal papers of Jim Thorpe. Their archival resources were invaluable in bringing his story to life. Special thanks to the Library of Congress for access to the Jim Thorpe Papers.

A portion of the proceeds from this book will be donated to the *Jim Thorpe Memorial Foundation,* a non-profit organization dedicated to preserving the legacy of one of America's greatest athletes.

About the Author

Orlo Robertson was an Associated Press sportswriter and editor. He authored a biography of a US Air Force pilot in the Korean War titled "Captain Bob." Additionally, his biographical focus points to an interest in human stories and character development, even within a factual framework. Orlo's writing style of factual reporting delivers his audience clear, concise, and factual accounts of his characters.

Table of Contents

Foreword
by Anita Thorpe

Ever since I began answering questions about my grandfather, Jim Thorpe, people have always asked: Did you know him? What was he like? Do you have any stories?

Unfortunately, I never had the chance to meet him—he passed away in 1953, before I was born. But over the years, learning about the man behind the legend has felt like unwrapping gift after gift. With each new discovery, I have gotten closer to understanding who Jim Thorpe truly was.

This book invites you to join Associated Press sportswriter Orlo Robertson and Jim Thorpe himself as they share stories filled with the passion and enthusiasm only true sports fans can bring. Their chemistry leaps off the page, reminiscent of two die-hard fans reliving the thrill of a big game—celebrating victories, mourning defeats, and honoring the spirit of competition.

It has been an incredible honor to carry my grandfather's name and to help share the legacy he left behind—not just for our family, but for all who admire courage, perseverance, and greatness. Jim Thorpe was more than an athlete; he was a trailblazer. America's first multi-sport superstar, he is still the only person in history to have won both the Olympic decathlon and pentathlon. Today, an NFL coach seeking wisdom might study the strategies of Pop

Warner—and in doing so, inevitably meet the leadership, grit, and passion of Jim Thorpe.

After winning Olympic gold, researchers at the Carlisle Indian School conducted a study of Jim Thorpe's physique using anthropometric measurements. The results were surprising: he wasn't particularly large or physically imposing. His shoulders were narrow, his chest was of average size, but the muscles above his knees, especially in his thighs, stood out as exceptionally well-developed. Yet, what no measuring tool could capture was the true source of his greatness—his spirit. That inner strength could not be quantified or explained by science.

But you can begin to understand it—his spirit—if you try to step into his shoes. Jim Thorpe used visualization to elevate his performance, mentally picturing himself out-jumping or out-running others before physically doing it. He was a keen observer, learning by watching and then refining what he saw. His method was not just physical—it was deeply intuitive. What some outsiders misinterpreted as laziness—his midday naps or quiet moments of rest—were rooted in Indigenous traditions that emphasized conserving energy and living in harmony with the body's natural rhythms.

Jim Thorpe lived authentically. If something did not feel right, he changed it. He ran away from school to find his own path. He left situations that did not honor his worth. He signed his real name on contracts when others recommended deception to skirt the Amateur Athletic Association's rules. He led by example, displaying sportsmanship during a time when betting scandals, bribery, and racism plagued the leagues. He helped change society—paving the way for future minority athletes—and became the first president of what is now the NFL: the American Professional Football Association.

His story has been challenged, rewritten, and reclaimed over time—thanks to tireless advocacy from his family, supporters, and even lawmakers. On January 18, 1983, the International Olympic Committee returned his medals—not the originals, but replicas. Then, in 2022, they officially restored him as the sole winner of the 1912 Olympic decathlon and pentathlon, after renewed efforts and petitions from his advocates.

Still, questions remain. Will his original trophies ever be returned to his family or nation, as he wished?

You may notice that some details in this book no longer align with the most current research. These passages remain unedited, honoring the voice and context in which they were first told —not out of oversight, but out of respect. I would not have corrected my grandfather then, and I will not now.

The original gold medals were given to the runners-up: Ferdinand Bie of Norway (pentathlon) and Hugo Wieslander of Sweden (decathlon). Mr. Bie's medal was reported stolen in 1980 and remains missing. Mr. Wieslander donated his medal to the Malmö Sports Museum in Sweden. The Challenge Prizes that once belonged to Jim Thorpe were returned in 1913 and passed on to Bie and Wieslander. These items now reside in the Olympic Museum in Lausanne.

According to the 1912 Stockholm Games report, Challenge Prizes were never the athletes' property. All winners were required to return them before the next Games, scheduled for 1916, which were canceled due to World War I. The tradition of awarding Challenge Prizes ended shortly after, and they were preserved in the Olympic Museum.

And so, we continue the journey. Jim Thorpe's legacy endures—not just in medals or trophies, but in the stories, spirit, and inspiration he left behind.

Chapter One

Flashbacks

1907, Carlisle, Pa., Indiana Institute ---A husky lad clad in overalls and ordinary shoes walked out of a workshop and watched with open eyes as several athletes practiced the high jump. They were missing at five feet, eight inches.

Modestly, the 17-year-old youth asked permission to try his luck; several inches of daylight showed under his pants as he snaked over the bamboo bar. Among those who saw him and blinked was Glen Scobie (Pop) Warner, son of a Springfield, Ill., farmer who directed the Indians' athletics.

The lad was James Francis Thorpe, and that leap over the high jump bar was to start him on his way to international fame with Warner as the guiding hand.

1912 Stockholm, Sweden---The Olympics were over. Jim Thorpe had won both the decathlon and pentathlon. The 24-year-old Indian mounted the podium, hung his head in bashfulness, and heard King Gustav V of Sweden say:

"You, sir, are the greatest athlete in the world."

1912, U.S. Military Academy, West Point, N.Y. –Army kicked off to start the second half of the football game between the powerful cadets and the high-riding Carlisle Indians. Thorpe gathered the ball in on the 90—yard line and ran all the way for a touchdown. But there was an offside penalty, and Army kicked off again, this time to the five-yard stripe. And once more, Thorpe tucked the ball under his arm and headed downfield, racing 95 yards for a touchdown that counted this time. Carlisle won 27-6 with Jim accounting for 22 points.

1950, The United States—Nearly 400 of the nation's sports writers and sportscasters, in a poll conducted by The Associated Press, voted James Francis Thorpe the outstanding All-Around Athlete and the No. 1 football player of the century.

Chapter Two

And now, as Jim, at 62, looks back over a life that has been as full as one man could want, her picks those four events as the ones he most wants to remember.

There are stories about the athletic feats of this Sac and Fox Indian that have almost become legendary in athletic circles. There are stories of a man, Hiram Thorpe, who was the top in every sport in which he participated—and there were only a few in which he didn't try his hand. Stories of how, on the downgrade, he reached the stage where he dug ditches to provide food and shelter for his family. Stories of how he didn't have enough money to purchase a ticket for the 1932 Olympics in Los Angeles, but friends quickly rectified that situation.

Stories of how he gave way to overindulgence in liquor to drown out the bad breaks of the past.

But the tale doesn't end there, fortunately for the once might Indian realized where he was heading, took hold of himself and said:

"An Indian can't drink, nor can an Irishman; I'm a little of both, so no more hard stuff for me."

That was four years ago, and Jim has kept that promise to himself. His many friends, realizing the battle he was making, helped him achieve victory. But most of all, it was a triumph for James Francis, who won as he overcame his athletic rivals for 22 years.

Maybe a letter received a few years ago from a Raleigh, South Carolina, youngster had something to do with it, because if Jim has one weakness, it is for kids. One of his ambitions is to establish a foundation that will provide proper recreational activities for the underprivileged youth of America.

Jim had been struck down by a heart attack while working for the Ford Motor company in Detroit. The South Carolina boy wrote:

"Dear Mr. Thorpe, I was listening to the radio tonight when Bill Stern said something about America's greatest athlete being sick."

"I knew right away who he was talking about. He said you had a heart attack, Mr. Thorpe. He said that Knute Rockne once said that you couldn't be stopped, and I know that you won't be stopped now. I am only a boy of 15, and I know that you have never heard of me, but as one sports lover to another, please, Mr. Thorpe, get well. If you get well, sports will mean more to me and millions of other American boys who will know that a true sportsman can pull through anything."

Jim himself doesn't quite understand all the new interest taken in him since the Associated Press poll. In his artless, simple-hearted way, he accepted the accolades of the public years ago and apparently forgot it.

He does know that wherever he goes, he seems to bring a glow into the lives of those he meets. Total strangers flock around with shining eyes, walk up to him, and say, "I just want to shake the hand of Jim Thorpe."

There's the incident of a man who saw Jim in the huge Pennsylvania Railroad Station in Philadelphia not so long ago. The man in his thirties greeted him with:

"You're Jim Thorpe, aren't you?"

Jim nodded, and the stranger went on:

"I'm from Oklahoma City and always wanted to meet my state's greatest."

A youngster of 12 was excused from school so he could meet Jim and get his autograph. The autograph was proof that he wasn't trying to pull a fast one on his teacher.

Jim stopped at a little Pennsylvania roadside restaurant for his favorite dish of ham and eggs. Across the street was a school. Soon, the word got around that the famous Indian was nearby, and within a few minutes, the restaurant was crowded with boys seeking autographs.

There is a certain grandeur about Jim, be it in a crowd or on his feet, giving a talk on his past experiences and clean living. He is not a polished speaker, but with quiet dignity, the simple homespun Indian speaks in the only language he knows—with plainness and truthfulness.

Jim Thorpe is not a complex man. He was weak in some respects, pliable, irresponsible, and sometimes unruly during his youth. But the white man's style of using cleverly evasive words, lies, flimflam, and shrewd scheming never was Jim's. He has always believed that a thing should be said so everybody could understand it, and that a promise is a promise.

The one bitter drug in Jim's life –one that he'll never forget—is against the athletics authorities that took away from him the $50,000 in trophies he won in the 1912 Olympics after sweeping the decathlon and pentathlon.

Jim was ruled a professional after the games because he played organized ball down in the south for a mere pittance of $60.00. The trophies were presented to him by the King of Sweden and the Czar of Russia; they are now lodged in Switzerland, the winners of second place in both events having refused them.

To this day, Jim can't understand why they were taken from him, for after all, he says he made no pretense of playing baseball under an assumed name as did other college athletes for the north, and the money furnished him nothing more than enough to live on.

Repeated attempts have been made to regain the trophies for Thorpe, but without success. He hoped that a committee of prominent men would get together and get some action, even to the extent that they are brought back to this country to raise funds for some charity or his proposed foundation.

As it is Jim, he has only pictures of the huge trophies and his memories to remind him of those triumphant days in Stockholm.

Perhaps Jim's feelings on the matter are best understood by the letter that he wrote to Commissioner James E. Sullivan of the Amateur Athletic Union of America. It was written after Thorpe played football at Carlisle in the fall of 1912 and was preparing for the 1913 track and field season.

Here is the letter dated Jan. 27, 1913:

"Dear Sir, when the interview with Mr. Clancy, stating that I had played baseball on the Winston-Salem team, was shown to me, I told Mr. Warner that it was not true, and in fact, I did not play on that team.

But so much has been said in the papers since then that I went to the school's authorities this morning and told them just what was in the stories.

I played baseball at Rock Mount and at Fayetteville, N.C., in the summer of 1909 and 1910 under my own name. On the same teams I played with were several college men from the north, who were earning money by ball playing during their vacations and who were regarded as amateurs at home.

I did not play for the money that was in it, but because I liked to play ball. I was not very wise to the ways of the world and did not realize that this was wrong, and it would make me a professional in track sports, although I learned from the other players that it would be better for me no to let anyone know that I was playing and for that reason I never told anyone at the school about it until today.

In the fall of 1911, I applied for readmission to this school and came back to continue my studies and take part in the school sports, and of course, I wanted to get on the Olympic team and take the trip to Stockholm.

I had Mr. Warner send in my application to register for the A.A.U. After I had answered the questions and signed it, I received my card allowing me to compete in the winter meets and other track sports.

I never realized until now what a big mistake I made by keeping it a secret about my ball playing, and I am sorry I did so. I hope I will be partly excused by the fact that I was simply an Indian schoolboy and did not know all about such things. In fact, I did not know that I was doing wrong because I was doing what I knew several other college men had done, except that they did not use their own names.

I have always liked sports and only played or ran races for the fun of the thing and never to earn any money. I have received offers amounting to thousands of dollars since my victories last summer, but I have turned them all down because I did not care to make money from my athletic skill.

I am very sorry, Mr. Sullivan, to have it all spoiled in this way, and I hope the amateur union and the people will not be too hard in judging me. "

Yours truly

(signed) James Thorpe.

Chapter Three

Jim Becomes a Man

To best understand this man who was later to captivate the world with his athletic skill and leave an imprint in sports that'll never be forgotten, it is necessary to look back into his youth.

Jim Thorpe was only a skinny youngster of 12 at the time, but within a year, he was to prove to his exacting and often harsh father that he was a man. At the age when most youngsters have nothing more important on their minds than to romp and play, Jim was required to do a man's work on the ranch of his parents down in Oklahoma's Indian territory.

One morning, while seated at the breakfast table with his mother and father, the subject in discussion was who would go to the Sac and Fox Indian agency school to bring home two of Jim's sisters, Mary and Adeline.

Jim volunteered, but Hiram Thorpe, the father, replied:

"You can't go, you cannot be trusted with a team of horses."

The argument waxed hotter with young Jim declaring that if he was man enough to do all the hard ranch work required of him, he certainly was old enough and trustworthy enough to hitch up a team of horses to the buckboard and drive the few miles necessary to get his sisters.

His father became very angry and finally threw a cup at the lad. The cup hit Jim's plate, hurling food over the youngster. Jim rose, left the table, walked out of the house, and kept on walking until he reached the home of his grandfather at Yale, Oklahoma, about 40 miles away.

Jim was gone for almost a year. He obtained a job on a ranch near Amarillo, Texas, where he did what is known in cattle circles as line riding. The job is called for fixing fences, finding stray cattle, and generally doing the work of a grown ranch hand.

He received $75 a month and found (room and board). The work was hard and the hours long for a 12-year-old boy. But Jim stuck to it, saved his money, and accomplished what he had set out to do— to prove to his father that he was a man and could be trusted.

When Jim returned home, he was riding a big, roan horse with a good saddle and leading a team of work horses.

Jim's father said little, for he was a stubborn man, but from then on, Jim's stature as a person would be trusted to accomplish a job increased.

Now, having passed through the cycle that would be the envy of any man, Jim looks back to those childhood days and with a grin that is typically Jim Thorpe says:

"It was fun."

Jim, in one of his infrequent periods of reminiscing, relates the story of his first attempt at high diving while working on the Box X ranch that year.

Several of the cowhands, including Jim, were down in a pasture at the windmill, watering the cattle. There was a large water tank, about 10 feet high and some eight feet deep.

The day was hot and dry, and the conversation turned to swimming, diving, and how the cool water in the tank would feel. One of the men said:

"Jim, if you will go to the top of the windmill and dive into the tank, I will follow you."

Young Thorpe thought that would be fun, even though the windmill was approximately 45 feet in height. Jim yanked off his shoes, a few of his clothes, and climbed the tower, made his dive, and emerged laughing.

The man who had promoted the idea climbed to the top of the windmill, looked down at the water, and got cold feet. He refused to jump, whereupon the men on the ground grew their guns, for those were the days when cowhands carried firearms, peppered a few shots around their friend atop the windmill.

"Needless to say, Jim relates he was not long in getting off the top of the windmill, but it was feet first."

Horseback riding has always been second nature to an Indian, and Jim proved he was no exception while cow punching that year in Texas.

Mr. Armstrong, owner of the Box X, had given orders not to permit Jim on a wild or fractious horse. But during the roundup, the men gave Jim an especially vicious animal to ride—nobody else on the ranch had been able to handle the horse.

As Jim swung his legs across the saddle, the horse broke out in all his bag of tricks—bucking, standing, and rearing stiff-legged.

"Stay with him, kid", the cowhand shouted as they threw their hands in the air and yelled encouragement, and stay on Jim did, not once pulling leather.

That is the picture of the youth who, 12 years later, was to be called to the victor's podium at the 1912 Olympic games in Stockholm and hear from King Gustave V: "You, sir, are the greatest athlete in the world." And Jim, with an Indian's traditional stolidity, replied: "Thanks, King."

Since that eventful summer day, fate has not always been kind for the broad-shouldered Sac and Fox Indian through whose veins also flows blood of the hardy Irish.

But Jim prefers not to talk of the days he was down, even though his Olympic medals were taken from him when it was discovered he played pro bb for a mere $60.

He likes to recall the days when he ruled the intercollegiate football roost as a member of the fabulous Carlisle Indians under Glenn (Pop) Warner of the days when his Canton Bulldogs romped over the professional gridirons and the days when he played baseball with the New York Giants under the late John McGraw and of the days when he thought nothing of winning six and seven events in dual track and field meets.

Thorpe was not without recognition during his athletic days, for he was twice named to the All-America football team by Walter Camp. His Olympic decathlon and pentathlon triumphs were victories of perfection achieved with no thought of establishing records.

But it remained for the sports writers and sports casters of radio to bestow probably the greatest honor on Thorpe after he had long passed his playing days.

No other athlete was close to Thorpe in the balloting conducted by The Associated Press for the No. 1 football player and the foremost all-around athlete of the last 50 years.

Yet this great honor made no change in the big Indian, whose favorite hobby is now, as always, sleep and eat. He was never one to exert any unnecessary energy.

"You know it took me nearly a month to make Jim understand the honor bestowed upon him by the writers," said Mrs. Thorpe, his third wife. "He's not dumb, understand, but he is so used to taking things for granted that the Associated Press poll made very little impression on him at first.

"Finally, I said to him, 'You big lug, don't you know this is the greatest honor that ever has been bestowed on an athlete?'"

With that contagious grin of his, Jim replied:

"I guess I must have been pretty good."

Chapter Four

The greatest accolade that can be awarded to a football player probably is:

"He's as good as Jim Thorpe in his prime."

Sometimes the word "better" is used, usually with tongue in cheek, for those who remember Jim at his best and who have followed the development of the later-day stars, consider the Sac and Fox Indian as the criterion by which all others are judged.

Admitting his one great fault, laziness, they can't agree that any one athlete had greater all-around ability, whether it be football, track and field, baseball, basketball, or lacrosse.

He was a good swimmer, although he never competed in the sport, wrestled, and when he took up golf more as a dare, he showed he could hit a golf ball better than the ordinary performer.

He had the natural ease and relaxation that goes toward making an athlete great. He defeated rules and training –a fact that often got him into trouble with coaches—but when the chips were down, there never was anybody greater.

Jim didn't like track and field at first, but it came to be his favorite sport.

"Liked it because I could take a snooze between each event."

And the story is told of his training for the Olympics in Stockholm. While lolling in a hammock, he asked one of his teammates to measure off 23 feet for the broad jump.

"Fine," said Jim after the 23 feet had been measured off. "That's my workout in the broad jump for the day."

Warner, with whom Jim rode to fame at Carlisle, once termed the Indian "a Saturday player who shirked practice, smoked on the sly and hated to buck the line, though he had few equals as a plunger."

Jim, to this day, says he couldn't see the use of using all that energy going through the line when he could go around the end and simply outrun the would-be tacklers.

He suffered from the Indians' traditional weakness for firewater. He learned to like liquor before he learned to use it in moderation. But because he is a man, he saw where liquor was leading him. On the comeback trail under the direction of Mrs. Thorpe, his wife, the Big Indian has shown he can leave liquor alone. And such has proved to his countless friends and admirers that he has conquered firewater just as he conquered sports years ago.

Although it was Warner who discovered Thorpe's athletic ability, he came by it naturally.

His father was a big bull of a man, weighing some 230 pounds, possessing tremendous physical energy. He was the best for miles around at running, jumping, and wrestling. And when he took young Jim on hunting trips, he set a pace that the youngster found hard to follow.

The father didn't know all about today's physical fitness programs of modern educational institutions, but in his own way, he believed in keeping fit and saw that his children did the same.

Jim, like his half-Irish, half-Indian father, was said to bear a strong resemblance to the famous Sac and Fox chieftain, Black Hawk. In later years, many Indians believed Thorpe to be a reincarnation of Black Hawk, of whom Jim was a direct descendant.

Black Hawk, who succeeded his father as head chief of the Sacs in 1788, was better known for the trouble he caused the federal government before peace was made in 1832. But the history of the tribe, now reduced to some 500 members, shows there was no better physicality. He was a true chieftain because he could outrun, outshoot, and outride any of his warriors.

When Black Hawks surrendered Aug. 27, 1832, he and nine other warriors were held for a time as hostages, and after being taken to several eastern cities, were confined in fortress Monroe until June 8, 1833. The Sac and Foxes under Chief Keokuk soon moved to a reservation near Fort Des Moines, Iowa, where Black Hawk died five years later. In later years, the Sac and Foxes were moved to the Indian territory, now the state of Oklahoma.

It was there that James Francis Thorpe was born in a one-room log farmhouse on the banks of the North Fork River near Prague on May 28, 1888. His mother, Charlotte View, was three-fourths Pottawatomie and one-fourth French—a blood mixture which, as Jim later said:

"Makes me a sort of a human Airedale."

Jim's mother gave him the Indian name of Wah-Tho-Huck (Bright Path). But to his father, the boy was always Jim.

Jim had a twin brother, Charles, who died at the age of eight. Other members of the Thorpe family were a half-brother and sister, Frank, Minnie, and George, his other brother by seven years and three younger children, Mary, Adeline, and Eddie.

Until Charles' death, the twins were inseparable as they lived the normal outdoor life of Indian children. They learned to fish, hunt, trap, and play the games that called for speed and endurance.

The Thorpes were far from a poor family. Hiram, with the help of Jim and the other children, farmed over 300 acres. At times, there were as many as 400 heads of cattle, horses, and hogs on the farm. It took plenty of food to keep the big family of husky Indians from becoming hungry.

At an early age, Jim learned, as did other Indian boys, to ride bareback on the half-wild range ponies, so his experience at the age of 12 in Texas was no accident. He recalls some of the most pleasant memories of his childhood when they would round up the colts on the open range and break them for riding.

When it came time for book learning, young Jim was sent to the old Sac and Fox agency school about 20 miles from his home.

And the school, indirectly, led to Jim's first long foot race. He had attended the school for about four years when he became bored with books and perhaps was a bit lonely.

Whatever the reason, Jim ran away and walked all the way home. The father, suspecting what had happened when he saw Jim coming, was standing at the door with a willowy switch in hand.

Jim, to this day, maintains that as soon as he saw his father and the switch, he turned around and ran every step of the way back to school.

But the school couldn't hold Jim. After a few more escapades, his father decided to send him so far away that he couldn't walk home. The destination was Haskell Institute at Lawrence, Kansas.

It was at Haskell that Jim received his first glimpse of football as played by a high-class team. Haskell, in those days, was well known as a power on the gridiron. Too small and young for the varsity, Jim learned something about the sport on an informal class team.

He also picked up the rudiments of baseball and the then-new game of basketball. Although small, he took to them like they were cousins.

But Haskell couldn't hold Thorpe, either. Hearing that his father was ill, he again ran away and somehow managed to find his way back home. His mother died shortly afterwards, and Jim never returned to Haskell.

Jim was 15 in 1903 when an agent from the Carlisle Institute in Pennsylvania came through the Indian territory looking for prospective students.

Thorpe's father, having noticed in Jim's runaway escapades his desire to roam and see the country, readily gave his consent for the youngster to make the long trip.

The United States Indian Industrial School at Carlisle was established in 1879 on an abandoned army post at the urging of R.H. Pratt, an army officer who had made a reputation in the Indian wars.

The Indians from Carlisle won their football reputation playing college teams, but academically, it was on a high school level. There were no scholastic requirements, and no classes above the 12th grade; it wasn't unusual for an athlete, competing against college men, to be in the fourth grade.

Thorpe himself was 24 in his last year at school, and today he doesn't recall how far he had progressed in education on the basis of today's academic standings.

Carlisle also had a system through which students were sent out during vacation periods and often for as long as a year to live with families and work with them. During the heyday of Warner's football teams at Carlisle, it was strongly hinted, but never proved, that some of the "Indians" strongly resembled some of the husky Pennsylvania Dutch boys of the surrounding area.

But apparently, the Harvard and Pennsylvanians were such sticklers as they are today for the academic standing of their rivals to be on the proper plane. Or it could have been that they thought Warner's poor little Indians were pushovers. But if that was so, it didn't take them long to discover otherwise.

Jim's father died shortly after he enrolled at Carlisle, and in the summer of 1904, the young Indian was sent out to live with families in Pennsylvania. He received five to eight dollars a month and his keep as a farm hand, gardener, and cook.

By the time fall of 1906 had rolled around, Jim had grown enough to become a member of a shop eleven, which won what was equivalent to the intramural football championship of the school.

His play on the shop team was good enough to earn him a spot on the varsity scrubs. Jim recalls they were called the "hotshots" --- a motley group of youngsters dressed in castoff, ill-fitting uniforms.

Jim tells the amusing tale of his own first appearance on a Carlisle football field.

"My pants were fastened under my armpits and hung down to my ankles. The jersey was big enough for two Jim Thorpes, and the shoes were so large that I had to strap them on to keep them from coming off."

There was nothing about me to encourage a football coach to take a second look, Jim relates with the Thorpe grin.

But within another few months, the athletic career of James Francis Thorpe really began to unfold.

It was the impromptu high jumping effort, related at the start of this book, that attracted Glenn Scobey Warner to the man destined to become the world's greatest athlete.

There are several versions of just how Jim got his chance at the high jump, but as Thorpe, himself, recalls, he had walked out of a workshop and was cleaning up the athletic field when he noticed some of the older boys at the high jump pit.

When they had failed to clear the bar at five feet, eight inches, Jim asked permission to try it. Wearing dungarees and an old pair of tennis sneakers, he went over with inches to spare, much to the amazement of Warner.

The ambitious Carlisle coach lost no time seeing that Jim came out for varsity sports, and as Jim showed adeptness at every event, it wasn't long before Warner was dreaming of an all-around Olympic championship title for the youth who like nothing better than to run and jump. There was nothing that the coach asked Jim to do that the Indian didn't do well.

Chapter Five

No story of Jim Thorpe would be complete without a chapter on Pop Warner—the man who saw the Sac and Fox Indian high jumping on the Carlisle campus and guided him through his intercollegiate and football career.

The mutual admiration of Warner for Thorpe and for Warner never ceased. Pop, living out the closing years of his life on the Pacific coast, calls Thorpe the greatest athlete he ever coached. Jim, in turn, bows to Pop as the foremost coach of football.

Warner, somewhat of an athlete himself at Cornell, started his coaching at the University of Iowa and the University of Georgia in 1895. After pre-season coaching at Iowa, he was contracted to direct the Georgia football team for ten weeks. His salary was $35. The next year, he received an increase of $5 but had to coach an additional two weeks.

After returning to Cornell for a couple of years, he arrived at Carlisle in 1899 to take over the coaching of the Indians. Even then, the red men were developing something of a reputation on the gridiron, even though the game was still largely for big brutes. The Indians were not large, but they were agile and fast—a factor that Warner put to good use.

Before Warner's arrival, the Indians had given mighty Harvard a scare before losing 4-0 in 1896, and two years later were beaten only 11-5 by a Harvard team that was rated as national champions.

Warner's debut as coach at Carlisle was about the time when a group of coaches were doing much to change the style of play from strictly brute force to one of speed and elusiveness.

Fielding Yost developed his "point-a-minute" teams at the University of Michigan soon after the start of the century, with such rugged stars as Germany Schultz and Willie Heston going down in the football history books.

Amos Alonzo Stagg was making the name of the University of Chicago feared on every gridiron. Those were the days when smart, elusive Walter Eckersall and huge Tiny Maxwell were attending school down in Chicago's Midway.

Percy Haughton, later to become Harvard's most famous coach, was developing his system at Cornell. John W. Heisman, Dan McGuigan, Dr. Henry L. Williams, designer of the "Minnesota shift", Gil Dobie, and others were members of the coaching fraternity, which was largely responsible for the opening up of the game.

Warner was said to have done more than any other to change the rules. And probably out of necessity, for he saw in the Indians of Carlisle the material for the development of trick plays.

It was at Carlisle in 1903 that Warner produced the "hidden ball" play—a play that astounded Harvard and eastern football fans. Pop had seen it used at Auburn in 1895 and stored it away in his fertile mind for use at an opportune time.

When Harvard kicked off to start the second half, the Carlisle quarterback, named Johnson, caught the ball. The Indians huddled around him as if to form a flying wedge. Instead, they shoved the ball inside the back of Dillon's jersey. They then fanned out across the field, running with arms outstretched.

The bewildered Harvard players didn't know what had happened until Dillon crossed the goal line. It almost won the game, too, but Harvard finally nosed out the Indians 11-10.

"The public expects the Indians to employ trickery, and we try to oblige," Warner explained later in defending the play.

Warner almost didn't land at Carlisle. If an offer from Minnesota had arrived a few hours earlier, this chapter might have been omitted.

The offers from the two schools arrived within a few hours of each other, but Carlisle was first. Warner, too, admired the Indians' willingness to take on all comers.

The Carlisle job also offered the young coach a chance to buy in on the gate receipts. With no wealthy or sizeable students or alumni bodies to furnish financial support and no nearby large city to supply paying customers, Carlisle played all its games on the road.

They travelled from coast to coast under Warner, and Pop never got the worst of the dickering for a cut in the gate receipts.

Warner likes to relate the story of the day when his team trotted out on a field where the stadium was filled with supporters of the home team. The fans were shouting and singing college songs. Not a voice was raised in support of the Indians.

Man-Afraid-of-a-Bear (Sam McLain) surveyed the scene, turned to Warner, and calmly remarked:

"Good thing it isn't a singing contest, hey, Pop?"

Every year was not a good one for Warner at Carlisle, but he won one of his best elevens in his first year at the Institute. The Indians, who whipped almost everything in the east, were the only ones to score on Harvard that year, losing 22-10, and ended the season by beating the University of California 2-0 in the first intersectional game played on the West Coast.

On that team, Warner had such outstanding performers as Isaac Seneca, named by Walter Camp to a halfback slot on the All-America; Wheelock, a tackle whom Camp placed on his second All-America; and Frank Hudson, a 138-pound quarterback who was a third team selection.

Warner left Carlisle in 1904 for Cornell but was back in 1907— in time to discover Thorpe and lead the Indians in an area of football that called for more open play, forward passing, and long runs.

Two years before Warner's return to the Carlisle campus, football was on its way out as an intercollegiate sport. Several players were killed. Many more were seriously injured, and an outcry over the brutality of the sport spread over the nation. Columbia, Northwestern, and several smaller schools dropped the game. California and Stanford turned to the English rugby game.

President Theodore Roosevelt, a great lover of sports, stepped into the situation. He warned college leaders they must find a way to open the game to eliminate the slugging, the brutality, and the dirty playing, or the game would fail to exist.

Shortly afterwards, 28 Universities and Colleges formed the Intercollegiate Football Conference, the predecessor of the present National Collegiate Athletic Association.

Walter Camp proposed two of the most radical changes adopted by the rules committee. The distance to be gained on three downs was increased by five to 10 yards. The forward pass was introduced. Playing time was also reduced from 70 to 60 minutes. Rules curtailing roughness were enacted, and six men on the offensive team were required to be on the line of scrimmage.

And so it was into this new game, ideally suited to the talents of the Indian players, that Thorpe made his debut as a varsity player in 1907.

Warner's wing-back system called for a powerful left halfback who could sweep the ends, buck through the middle, slice off the tackles, and punt as well. After the departure of Seneca, there was nobody to answer that description at the Indian school until Thorpe arrived.

Weighing 155 pounds by the fall of 1907, Jim had managed to make the scrub team. Football was so new to him that in scrimmages, he would run right over his interference, often spilling himself.

Warner, busy preparing for another tough schedule, caught only flashes of Thorpe's speed until one day he yelled at the varsity:

"Get mean smack 'em down. Bang them so hard they don't get up."

Thorpe was downfield catching punts and returning them against defensive tacklers. He took one of the kicks, tucked the ball to his side, broke into his bounding, swerving stride, and headed downfield.

One man bounced off him, and so did another. Two grabbed at empty air. Jim pulled up at the other end of the field with a wide grin on his face. It was his first big thrill out of the game.

"No, no, not that way!" he recalls an assistant coach yelling. "This is tackling practice, understand?"

Thorpe looked at the coach, deadpanned, and said:

"Nobody tackles Jim."

Actually, he said later, "I was afraid if the big fellows got hold of me, they'd break me in half."

"So, I ran and ran and dodged this way and that and finally I ran across the goal line," he added."

That feat earned him a place on the varsity bench, but he didn't see action until the game against the University of Pennsylvania. That was after the Indians had trampled Susquehanna 91-0, Lebanon Valley 40-0, Villanova 10-0, and Bucknell 15-0.

When halfback Albert Payne was injured during the Penn game, Warner gave Thorpe the nod. Jim didn't even know all the signals.

He was given the ball on the first play, but was so excited that he left his interference and ran the wrong way. Naturally, he was dumped for a big loss.

But on the next play, his signal was called again. This time, the speedy, elusive Sac and Fox youngster outran everyone, including his blockers, as he sped around the end for a 45-yard touchdown.

Warner's eyes popped as he counted the Pennsylvania boys flat on their stomachs behind Thorpe. There were seven who had tried and failed to tackle the galloping Thorpe.

"That's fun," Thorpe told his startled teammates in a huddle. "Give it to Jim again."

They fed the ball to him, and a bit later, he was loose again, running 85 yards through the floundering University of Pennsylvania eleven for another touchdown.

To this day, Warner likes to recall Thorpe's early days on the football field.

"Hell's bells, " he said. "Jim was lazy, didn't like to practice, and he gave out his best effort only when he felt like it, and that was about 40 percent of the time. Football was just a good time for Jim. I never saw him snarl, and mostly he just laughed, talked to the other team, and enjoyed himself. But, even at that, you couldn't keep him on the bench."

"He had a natural change of pace that just floated him past the defense. His reactions were so fast that sometimes you couldn't follow him with your eyes. Punishment didn't mean a thing to him. He was fearless, and he hit so hard that the other fellows got almost all the bruises."

Payne's injury caused him to drop out of school, and Thorpe got an opportunity after that to play regularly.

Despite his great flashy running against Pennsylvania, this growing youngster, now weighing 170 pounds, was overshadowed by such great backs as Albert Exendine, Pete Hauser, Frank Mount Pleasant, and Mike Balenti. Exendine later was a successful coach at Georgetown, Washington State, Occidental College, and Oklahoma A. & M.

Warner later called his 1907 team his greatest at Carlisle. The only defeat in 11 games that year was a 16-0 setback by Princeton. And incidentally, it was in the Princeton game that Thorpe's punting first began to attract attention.

The Indians, with a tricky attack, beat Harvard for the first time, 23-15, as Mount Pleasant ran 85 yards for one touchdown and set up two others with passes. They also whipped Penn State, Syracuse, Minnesota, and the University of Chicago.

Warner has always regarded Hauser as one of his greatest players.

It was Hauser, who helped in a game with a painful injury, who answered Warner's question with a remark that has almost become a classic wherever football stories are told. Warner asked Pete what happened.

"Same old thing," said Hauser. "They kneed me."

"What did you say? Did you say anything?" asked Warner.

"Yes, I said: 'Who's the savage now?'"

Chapter Six

Before the 1908 football season rolled around and Jim really began to make the name of Thorpe feared on the gridiron, the husky Redman embarked on a track and field career that paralleled his football feats for worldwide recognition.

As track coach, Warner figured he had a pretty good high jumper in Thorpe. But he probably didn't realize that Thorpe could perform equally well in other events. And for that matter, neither did Jim until, becoming weary of waiting around the field for his turn, he began to try them.

Thorpe's natural grace and ease were such that he almost automatically adopted the correct form when he tried a new event. The first time he saw a javelin, he picked up the spear and tossed it 120 feet. He whirled a 16-pound hammer around his head and heaved it out about the same distance. He strode over the high hurdles like he had been doing it all of his life without being told how to eliminate wasted motion.

His first competitive high jump was at the University of Pennsylvania relays, and he did six feet, one inch to tie for first place. By the toss of a coin, he won his first trophy, a gold watch. He failed to place in the hurdles but took third in the broad jump.

But before the spring track season was over, Jim had won the broad jump, both high and low hurdles, and the hammer throw in big meets.

Mike Murphy, a famed University of Pennsylvania coach who handled the 1912 Olympic track and field team, once asked:

"My God, Thorpe, how many events do you want to enter?"

Thorpe wasn't especially fond of track at first. Later, he said it was his favorite sport.

"I really get the most fun out of track because I wasn't looking for anything else in it," he explained. "I never cared about records. I just want to beat the other fellows, and when I got in front, I took it easy."

If Jim had been looking for anything else, he wouldn't have gotten it at Carlisle. The only awards he ever received for his performances were a watch, medals, or a suit of clothes.

Thorpe was the nearest possible thing to a one-man track team. Today, an athlete gets the headlines if he wins four or even three events in a meet. Jim thought nothing of winning five, six, and seven.

Tales of the mighty Thorpe often have grown with retelling, even though they were great enough in their origin. There is one, for instance, that he once won a track meet from Lafayette single-handedly.

Harold Anson Bruse, then Lafayette coach, says:

"There were four others, and they were pretty good too."

"They finished one, two in the half mile, and two miles."

What happened was that only Coach Warner and Thorpe were first seen when Bruce met them at the station.

"They'll be along," Warner assured Bruce when asked about the remainder of the team. And eventually they did come along to play an important part in the Indians' 71-31 victory.

Thorpe finished second in the 100-yard dash, his first event, then won the pole vault, high jump, broad jump, low hurdles, and pole vault. Perhaps he could have won the meet single-handed had it been necessary.

When he reported for football in the fall of 1908, Thorpe packed 180 pounds and was nearly six feet in height. Before ending his intercollegiate competition, he added another 22 pounds and grew to six feet one inch.

Carlisle, as usual, had a tough schedule —one that gave Thorpe the fullest opportunity to exhibit his ability as a ball carrier and kicker. He was selected for a third-team berth on Camp's All-America squad.

The Indians won ten, lost two, and tied one. The losses were to Harvard and Minnesota, and the deadlock was played against Pennsylvania.

Thorpe's first stellar performance came against Penn. State, when he kicked three field goals, one from 45 yards, for a 12-5 victory. He booted a 30-yard field goal in a 12-0 triumph over Syracuse and against Pennsylvania, led by the rugged Bill Hollenback, and out to avenge the 26-6 defeat of the previous year, Jim whirled 60 yards for the game-tying touchdowns. An injury kept him from kicking the next week against Navy, but he held the ball as Balenti booted four placements to win 16-6.

Then the Indians bowed to a rugged Harvard team, coached for the first time by Haughton. The Crimson of Harvard was led by All-

America Hamilton Fish, in later years a congressman from New York, and Joe Nourse.

The 1909 football guide said the Indians suffered "Stage Fright" as they lost 17-0, but they threatened the Harvard goal once with an early version of the Statue of Liberty play.

Thorpe faked a run around his right end, then passed to Hendricks, who reversed the field to threaten the left end, then tossed a lateral to Hauser, who reached Harvard's ten-yard line. After Thorpe was stopped on the four-yard mark, a pass was intercepted to avert a score.

The Indians turned back Pittsburgh 6-0 and then undertook one of the most remarkable trips ever made by a college football team. Western fans had heard of Thorpe and his mates and wanted to see them in action. Warner was willing to oblige—for a good guarantee.

Here's what they did in 15 days. They lost to Minnesota at Minneapolis 11-6 on a Saturday. The following Thursday, they were in St. Louis, where they beat St. Louis University 17-0. The next Tuesday found them in Lincoln, Neb., romping to a 37-6 victory over the University of Nebraska, and on Saturday, Hauser kicked two field goals to produce an 8-4 triumph over Denver University, the Rocky Mountain champions.

Jim had another successful track and field season in the spring of 1909 and then figured he had enough education. Warner was counting on Thorpe for a great gridiron season that fall, little realizing that an event would take place that would change the whole course of Jim Thorpe's life.

There is still a puzzled, wounded look on Jim's face as he relates the events that led to his being declared a professional and stripped of all his Olympic honors. It is the only bitter thought that Jim keeps.

After all these years, he can't see any real wrong in what he did. For after all, it was a common practice for college athletes to play professional baseball in the summer.

"My big mistake," says Jim, "Was playing under my own name."

As Jim relates the story, a group of his college friends, including Joe Libby and Jess Young Deer of Carlisle, were going to North Carolina that summer to play ball.

Having no particular desire to return to Oklahoma, Jim decided to go along with them and quickly landed a job with Rocky Mount of the Eastern Carolina League. The team was managed by Jim O'Connor.

In his first game, played at Raleigh, Thorpe was assigned to third base.

"I threw the ball so hard to first base," Jim recalls, "That O'Connor asked me if I would like to pitch the second game of the doubleheader. "

"It made no difference to me, just so I played. So, I pitched the second game and won 4-0. From then on, I was a pitcher."

Jim went on to win 23 out of 25 games for Rocky Mount. The Boston Braves heard of him and sent scouts, but by that time, it was 1910, and Jim had strained his arm. The Braves lost interest, and Thorpe moved to Fayetteville, where he played briefly. All this time, he never received more than $60 a month, out of which he had to pay all of his living expenses when the club was at home.

Thorpe returned home and whiled away the time hunting and fishing. Then one day came a letter from Warner, asking Jim to return to Carlisle.

"If you will come back to Carlisle and start training, I think you have a chance to make the Olympic team next year, "Warner wrote.

A few weeks later, Jim popped up at Carlisle with no idea that he was now a professional. Warner asked him where he had been, and Jim replied laconically:

"Playing ball.'

In those two years away from Carlisle, Jim had grown to six feet one and one-half inches, stripped to 185 pounds, and looked every inch an athlete.

Jim hadn't touched a football in two years, but in the Indians' opening game against Carlisle, he ripped off 17 points in 17 minutes. A week later, he blasted his way to three touchdowns against M. St. Mary's before Warner decided to let the second stringers take over.

Then came a much tougher foe in Georgetown. But with the Indians in front all the way, Warner didn't take the wraps off his swift halfback until late in the game. His stiff arm, a deadly defensive weapon, was all that Jim needed to scramble 40 yards for the final score in a 28-5 victory.

Harry Costello, who played against Thorpe that day and later with him on the Canton Bulldogs, recalls that Thorpe's kicking was sensational, and he was the hand-off man as Carlisle worked successfully the Statue of Liberty play.

Of Thorpe's gridiron prowess, Costello recently said: "Thorpe did everything. He could stand on the ten-yard line and kick a dozen punts over the other goal. He could outperform all of them at their own particular specialities. If he had a weakness, it was his over-anxiety to make every tackle. Occasionally, he would get sucked in, but not often."

Eastern sportswriters agreed that Carlisle had a fine team and one of the best backfield men in the east in Thorpe, but Jim wouldn't be able to call his shots against the more powerful elevens of Pittsburgh, Pennsylvania, and Syracuse.

The newspaper talk in those days was of small interest to Jim. He didn't start keeping a scrapbook until a year later and did no more than merely glance at his fan mail. Only when he thought someone was "Making fun of Jim" did he get aroused.

Informed he had been needled after the Georgetown game, Jim made sure that nobody would ever cast an aspersion at him but unleashed his full fury against Pittsburgh.

The Panthers were as tough as they came. They had openly boasted they would stop the big Indian. And they tried, cracking Thorpe two and three strong, piling on him when he was down and roughing him at every chance.

But through it all, the good-natured grin never left Jim's face.

"Next time—left tackle!" he would shout over the scrimmage line and then follow up with a tremendous blast at the designated spot.

"Unflustered by ruffian tactics, Thorpe paced Carlisle to an easy 17-0 victory over Pitt, " one sportswriter wrote.

Against Lafayette, Thorpe averaged over 70 yards on his kicks, scored two touchdowns and a field goal in a 19-0 triumph.

Then came the University of Pennsylvania, another one of the powers on the gridiron. Despite a stiff leg that put him temporarily on crutches preceding the game, Jim was all over the field. He set up two touchdowns, intercepted passes, came up from the deep secondary to break up Penn's line charges, applied blocks and tackles so savage they could be heard in the stands—in fact, he turned what figured to be a close ball game into another shutout, 16-0 for the Indians.

Harvard was next on the Indians' schedule. And Jim gave one of his great performances, although badly battered from the rugged handling he had received from the Pittsburgh and Pennsylvania players. One leg was heavily bandaged, and the other ankle was swollen.

But Jim, Warner said, "Had the heart of a lion. Although every movement must have been an agony, not once did he take time out."

The Crimson of Harvard had just been defeated by Princeton, and Harvard historians write off the Carlisle defeat as "Clearly a case of sacrificing a game to save a season." They could be right for a week, but later Harvard started its longest unbeaten streak.

Coach Percy Haughton had taken off for New Haven to scout Yale and left instructions with his assistants to use a substitute team against the Indians. The subs did play most of the game, almost on even terms with the Indians, but when the regulars came in during the last 12 minutes, their best effort was to block one of Thorpe's punts, enabling Bob Storer to get loose for the final touchdown.

Years later, however, Warner wrote a different version: "Because of his injuries and also because I know Harvard expected Jim to carry the ball on every play, I switched my plan of attack and used him only on interferences through the entire first half."

"Haughton threw in a brand-new team against us in the last quarter. As Jim saw the day going against us, he forgot his wrenched leg and sprained ankle and called for the ball."

"And get out of my way," he gritted. "I mean to do some real running."

"And how that Indian did run. After the game, one of the Harvard men told me that trying to stop the big Indian was like trying to stop a steam engine."

In either version, nothing could take away the glory of Jim Thorpe. He place-kicked four field goals that day to give Carlisle an 18-15 victory. He botched one for 22 yards in the first quarter, another from the 43-yard stripe in the second.

But Harvard's Paul Hollister matched the first three-pointer, and the Crimson made a touchdown to take a 9-6 lead. Carlisle came back with a touchdown of its own to regain the lead, and Thorpe made good on two more placements, the first one good for 34 yards and the last one from 48 yards out.

The next week, playing in the rain and mud, Jim had something of a letdown as Carlisle bowed 12-11 to Syracuse. Preston (Petey) Fogg, who captained the Syracuse team, remembers that day as one of the worst on which he ever played and that Thorpe had little success trying to run the ends.

Carlisle scored a quick touchdown, and Thorpe, apparently confident of a runaway triumph, missed the try for the extra point.

But Syracuse bounced back and took a 12-5 halftime lead. Thorpe scored again in the second half but couldn't get a third touchdown to make up for the missed extra point.

Fogg recalls that once, when he tackled Thorpe, Jim picked him up and said, "Nice work, kid." That was the kind of sportsman Jim was. He played for keeps, giving no quarter and taking no favors, but unless something was said or done to defame the name of Jim Thorpe or his teammates, the Sac and Fox Indian never lost his temper. He played the game for the sport of it.

Warner once said that Jim never extended himself further than to win and that he never gave more than one quarter of his ability. One can wonder just what the Oklahoma Indian would have accomplished had he given all of himself.

Victories over Johns Hopkins and Brown followed the Syracuse loss and enabled Carlisle to end the season with a record of 10 games won and one lost.

And there was no argument over Thorpe's place on the All-America backfield.

Chapter Seven

Jim was now riding high, and in his modest way, he liked it. If he was great on the gridiron in 1911, he was to become a household word by the time another football season rolled around.

Warner had promised Jim he would do his best to see that the big Indian made the 1912 Olympic team, and at the end of the 1911 football season, Pop set about to make his promise come true.

Jim was already in good physical condition, but his muscles were those of a football player. Warner coached the Indian tirelessly and had him compete in six or seven events through the winter and spring meets.

In one triangular meet against the University of Pennsylvania and Carnegie Tech, Thorpe won the high jump, shot put, and low hurdles, placed second in the high hurdles and broad jump, and third in the 100-yard dash.

And it didn't hurt the young Indian's chance of making the Olympic team by the fact that his performances were seen by Mike Murphy, the Penn and Olympic coach.

In the Olympic trials at the Polo Grounds in New York, Jim cleared the high jump bar at six feet, eight inches, only five-eighths of an inch under the world record, and qualified in the broad jump.

He was selected to represent the United States in the decathlon and pentathlon because of his known all-around ability. In those days, unlike today, separate qualification meets were not held in the decathlon and pentathlon.

Compared to today's world records, Thorpe's best performances, especially in the unfamiliar weight events, were not outstanding. But Thorpe, besides competing in many and specializing in none, wasn't going against modern records, present-day equipment, and modern coaching techniques, but for 1912, they were amazing and, taken as all-around feats, they are still amazing today.

One must also consider that Thorpe usually was not after records. His chief desire was to win.

Jim could run the 100-yard dash in 10 seconds, and Warner once caught him in 9.8 seconds in an exhibition, as compared to a 1912 record of 9.6 seconds. His best times for the high and low hurdles were only a fraction of a second away from the world standards, and his broad jump and shot-put marks were close to international record distances.

Some have said that Jim never took training seriously. Outwardly, he probably didn't, for Jim considered sports fun and not labor. But, known only to a few, Thorpe thought nothing of arising early in the morning and running 10, 20, or even 30 miles across country.

As a result, he was in superb condition by the time the athletes boarded the boat for Stockholm. While the other athlete toiled and sweated through training chores on shipboard, Jim lay in a hammock.

His training after the team reached Sweden wasn't much more strenuous. Under Warner's direction, Jim saw that his legs were kept in good condition.

Jim would jog a bit and announce he was all set.

One of the early events was the broad jump. The story is told that Jim put his hurdling shoes by the runway as a marker while he took his turn at the broad jump pit.

Somebody stole them. Jim offered to run the hurdles barefoot, but Warner quickly had heel spikes hammered into an extra pair of sprinting shoes. With this makeshift gear, he toed the starting line.

At the first flight of barriers, Jim stuck his chin in front and held the lead all the way, winning in 15.6. Thirty-six years and many technical advances in hurdling technique later, Bob Mathias won the same event in the London Olympics in 15.7

There have been stories that Jim sampled rather freely of the many varieties of Scandinavian spiritous liquors, but Thorpe, himself, emphatically denies it.

"Perhaps, I did celebrate a little afterwards," he says, "But not before or during the competition.'

Jim's work was done in three tremendous days. His performances will not be found in the Olympic books today, but here's what the so-called lazy Indian did against the world's top athletes:

Won four of five events in the pentathlon for a low score of seven points. He lost only in the javelin, finishing third to Sweden's Hugo Wieslander.

In the even more strenuous decathlon, Jim won the 110-meter-high hurdles in 15.6, the 1,500-meter run in 4:40.1, the shot put with a heave of 42 ft 5 ½ in., and the high jump with a leap of six ft. 1 ½ inches.

In addition, he was third in four other events and fourth in two more. His point total, under the scoring system then used, was an amazing 8,412.96 as compared to 7,724 for Wieslander, who finished second and was officially declared the winner over a year later when the American Amateur Athletic Union ruled Thorpe a professional because of his baseball activities.

Let's take a look at a table showing Thorpe's performances in the decathlon compared to the 1912 and today's records:

Event	Thorpe	1912 record	Modern Record
100 meters	11.2	10.6 (x)	10.2
Broad jump	22 ft. 6 3/5 in.	24 ft. 11 ¾ in.	26 ft. 8 ½ in.
High jump	6 ft 1 ½ in.	6 ft 7 in. (x)	6 ft. 11 in.
400 meters	52.2	48.2 (x)	46.0
Shot put	42 ft 5 ½ in.	51 ft.	57 ft. 1 in.
Discuss	121 ft. 3 ¾ in.	156 ft. 1 ¾ in (x)	180 ft. 2 ¾ in.
110-meter hurdles	15.6	15.0	13.7
Pole vault	10 ft. 8 in.	13 ft. 1 in. (x)	15 ft. 8 ½ in.
Javelin	149 ft. 11 ¼ in.	204 ft. 5 5/8 in. (x)	258 ft. 2 3/8 in.
1500 meters	4:40.1	3:55.8	3:43

(x) records set in 1912. Prior to 1912, the records were: 100 meters, 10.8; high jump, 6 ft 5 5/8 in.; 400 meters, 49.2; pole vault, 12 ft. 1/3 in.; javelin, 191 ft. 11 3/8 in.; discus, 141 ft. 4 ¾ in.

In the pentathlon, broad jumped 23 ft. 2 7/10 in., tossed the javelin 149 ft. 11 ¼ in., ran the 200 meters in 22.9, and the 1,500 meters in 4:44.8, and threw the discus 116 ft. 8 ½ in.

When he was called up to the victor's podium at the close of the games and presented the trophies—a bronze bust of King Gustav V of Sweden for his decathlon triumph and a gem-studded silver chalice presented by the Czar of Russia for winning the pentathlon, King Gustav told him:

"You, sir, are the greatest athlete in the world."

And Jim, with the Indian's traditional stolidity, replied:

"Thanks, King."

There is a story, which Jim half-way denies, that bears repeating, for it tells in few, simple words of the independence of the Indian.

As the ship was about to leave Sweden, bringing the United States athletes home, a representative of the King rushed aboard with word that His Majesty would like to see Thorpe.

While athletic bigwigs argued and pleaded with Jim to go see the King, Thorpe quietly replied:

"Tell the King I appreciate his invitation, but I'm sleepy."

Thorpe returned a hero to the nation. There was a parade amid packed throngs and flying ticker tape up the canyons they call streets in New York, another in Philadelphia, and the people of Carlisle and for miles around turned out to honor the youth that had brought fame to the Indian school.

Congressmen and cabinet members wrote him letters of congratulations, but the one that Jim covets most of all as he looks through his well-worn scrapbooks is one from William Howard Taft, president of the United States.

It reads:

"My dear sir:

I have much pleasure in congratulating you on account of your noteworthy victory at the Olympic Games in Stockholm. Your performance is one of which you may well be proud of. You have set a high standard of physical development, which is only attained by right living and right thinking, and your victory will serve as an incentive to all to improve those qualities which characterize the best type of American citizen.

It is my earnest wish that the future will bring you success in your chosen field of endeavor. "

With heartiest congratulations, I am.

Sincerely Yours,

W. H. Taft

Hundreds of offers to capitalize on his reputation poured in.

"One of them was for $1,500 a week to go on a stage tour, "recalls Jim. "They couldn't understand why I turned it down, but I wouldn't have been able to talk to people."

This naïve, unpolished prodigy from Oklahoma's sagebrush country never was much of a speech-maker, in that he had a command of big and flowery words. Yet today, he'll hold hundreds of children and adults alike spellbound with his simple and often ungrammatical account of his life.

Youth who know no more about Jim Thorpe than what they have read flock around him. Adults who lived in the Thorpe heyday speak with pride of the performance of the simple, trustful Indian, endowed with a magnificent body, and who asked but for one thing—a chance to play the games he loved.

So, it was a little wonder that it was a bewildered Indian who was ordered to return his medals on being declared a professional at the close of the 1912 football season. What had he done that was wrong? He had won these trophies—a king had given them to him, and now they wanted them back.

But Wieslander and F.R. Bie of Norway, second in the decathlon, refused to accept the trophies, saying:

"We didn't win the Olympic pentathlon and decathlon, Thorpe did. We don't know what your rules are in regard to amateurism, but we do know, having competed against him, that Thorpe is the greatest athlete in the world."

Where the credit—if that's what it should be called—for the startling disclosure that Thorpe had played professional baseball in 1909 belongs is uncertain. Several sports writers, among them Francis Albertanti, now a sports publicist, and the late Ed Moss, long-time secretary of the United States Lawn Tennis Association, told the same story.

They had seen a reference to Thorpe's ball playing while reading out-of-town newspapers and had recognized it as big news. Still another version is that a former baseball player, who was writing sports for a Worcester, Mass., newspaper, saw Jim's picture and recognized his former Fayetteville teammate.

All of the stories could have been true. For it also is true that during the Olympics, southern newspapers carried stories about Thorpe with references to his baseball connection in the Carolinas. Nobody thought much about it, nor did anyone call it to the attention of James E. Sullivan, the A.A.U. Secretary.

Chapter Eight

But before the disclosure that changed Thorpe's life, Jim returned to Carlisle for his last and greatest season of college football. If any one football player dominated the gridiron sport, Thorpe did it in 1912.

If ever an unstoppable back broke from scrimmage, it was Thorpe in the months after the Olympics. Walter Camp, who had named Jim to his 1911 All-America team, was never known to be at a loss for an adjective. But even he was stuck for descriptive words.

"On a clear day, I have seen him kick a football, including rolling, out of sight," wrote Camp.

Carlisle won 12 games, lost one, and tied one that season. Teamed with Thorpe were such great Indian stars as Gus Welch; Begie, the center; Pete Calac, a fine fullback; and Joe Guyon, who went from Carlisle to further football games at Georgia Tech.

Thorpe scored 25 of his team's 66 touchdowns, kicked field goals, and extra points. All of which added up to 198 points in 14 games. That total has never been matched against major competition, although in 1926, an Indian, Mayes McLain, scored 253 points for Haskell—the same school attended by Thorpe briefly in his younger days.

Jim was captain of the 1912 team, confident of his ability and harder to handle than ever. At times, he was maddening to Warner, but when he felt like playing or when he was mad, he was practically unstoppable.

Welsh made a specialty in the after years of convulsing audiences by telling of his first game with Old Jim. Gus was a blocking back, and as they went on the field, he asked what to do if he missed his block on the opposing end.

"Keep right on running, go down and get the halfback," Jim said.

As Welch explains:

"The ball went to Thorpe, and I went to take out the end. I missed him, so I kept on and went after the halfback. I missed him, too, so I thought I might as well go down and take the safety man. He side-stepped me. Then I looked around, and there was Jim right beside me. So, we went over the line together for the touchdown."

In an early-season game, Carlisle was backed to its goal line with Jim in punt formation. The Carlisle center passed the ball high over his head. Jim raced back, retrieving the ball 20 yards behind his goal.

A wave of tacklers bore down on him, sure of crushing the great Thorpe at last. Instead of trying to duck, Jim lowered his head and crashed straight ahead. Bodies bounced like ping-pong balls. Jim was staggered, knocked to his knees, but he kept going, winding up 120 yards away for a touchdown.

The Indians' one-tie game that year was a scoreless affair against Washington and Jefferson, the team that later was to receive the Rose Bowl bid. The Presidents of W. & J. yielded plenty of yardage to Jim and his teammates, but no touchdowns.

Thorpe blamed himself for not scoring, and the story is that he tried to drown his grief in beer. When the team gathered for dinner before leaving for Carlisle. Warner counted noses. Jim was missing.

Nobody wanted to squeal on Jim, but Welch, who was Thorpe's best pal, finally admitted he had left the Indians' star in a bar down the street. Warner found Jim sitting hunched over some empty beer bottles, trying to forget that rotten ball game.

Back at Carlisle, Warner gave Jim the granddaddy of all dressing-downs.

"It's a hell of a note for a great public figure, an Olympic champion, to make a fool of himself like that, Warner said. Thorpe nodded glumly.

"You'll have to apologize to the squad," ordered Warner. "Otherwise, you can't play ball for me."

At a special meeting, Jim got up and stammered his regrets, a humble speech in which he said:

"By golly, I'll never take another drink of beer!" "Or anything else," Warner came back. "Yep, or anything else," added Jim.

Warner's most trouble with Thorpe, however, was to keep the Indian keyed up so he would play his best.

The veteran coach tells the story of the game against Syracuse, which had beaten the Indians 12-11 in 1911. The Redmen were stopped cold in the first half. Thorpe's favorite style of running the ends wasn't working in the rain and mud.

At halftime, Warner stalked into the dressing room:

"We're not getting anywhere on those end runs," he growled. "If we're going to win, you've got to stop going wide and hit 'em up the middle."

Thorpe was unconcerned. He had his own football philosophy, and it wasn't based on hard work.

"Aw, what's the use of running through 'em," he said, "When you can run around 'em?"

That was all that Warner needed. In blistering works, he told his star what he thought of loafers who wanted to win the easy way. The grin disappeared from Thorpe's face. And it was tough on Syracuse.

Warner learned in the second half, if he didn't already realize it, that Thorpe was without peer in bucking the line. Driving, hammering, digging out chunks of yardage, Jim scored three touchdowns and set up two others. Final score: Carlisle 33, Syracuse 0.

The Indians even took a fling at the Canadian style of football, meeting an All-Star team assembled for an exhibition in Toronto. Thorpe and his mates won 49-1. They played the Canadians under their own rules in the last period and outscored them 5 to 1.

A column from an unidentified Canadian newspaper in Thorpe's scrapbook has this to say of the game:

"The Carlisle Indians were an object lesson at Varsity yesterday. American college teams were supposed to consist of so much beef and brawn, and there they came along, showing the highest kind of football skill. Most of the sharps went away from the stadium with the idea that the superior of Thorpe had not been seen in action in these parts. He had everything, including speed, strength, and ability to punt, drop, place pass, catch, tackle, besides displaying remarkable coolness and the best of judgement."

"The students cheered Thorpe from the start and were not satisfied until Dutch McPherson, the cheerleader, induced the Carlisle leader to come close. He stood stoically like a statue in front of the stand, accepted the cheers, bowed and smiled, and then loped back to his position where he continued to catch the punts in the palms of his hands and boot back spirals a good 75 yards."

But through all this, there were still some sportswriters, especially in New York, who doubted where Thorpe was all the headlines said. But they, too, were convinced at West Point when the Indians, with Thorpe at the peak of his game, whipped the Cadets 27-6.

Thorpe scored 22 of the Indians' points, and the next morning, the New York Tribune had this to say:

"Captain Jim Thorpe, the world's greatest all-around athlete, and noted as one of the greatest football players of all time, was the star of the game. His running with the ball was a revelation. Startling like a streak, he shot through the line, scattering tacklers to all sides of him. It was just before he was tackled or hit that Thorpe displayed his hardest running, and more than once it took a half-dozen men to drag him to earth."

"Not alone in carrying the ball was the value of Thorpe to his team show, but when Welch called for plunges into the line, Thorpe charged in and ripped great holes in the defense; he made it possible for the other backs to crash through."

The 1913 "Howitzer", Cadet yearbook, added another tribute:

"It was soon evident that the visitors, with the most powerful offense imaginable and an invulnerable defense, were sure to beat us. Their interference was perfect, and the running game of Thorpe was by far the most wonderful and spectacular ever seen on our field."

It was in that game that Thorpe blocked Leland Devere, Army's All-America tackle, so hard and so often that the Cadet captain lost his temper and was ordered out of the game for slugging.

Jim himself really had a day at his favorite sport.

Another story is that when the Indians were forced back near their goal, Thorpe whispered to an official:

"They think I'm going to kick, but I ain't."

He grabbed the ball and ran 80 yards before he was hauled down.

This is the game that stands out most of all in Thorpe's mind. As he thinks back over his athletic days, he likes nothing better than to tell of how he ran back two successive kickoffs for touchdowns, but only one counted.

But let Jim tell the story:

"It was the start of the second half. The Army boys kicked off. I took the ball on the 10-yard line and ran right down the middle of the field, all the way for a touchdown. But there was a penalty, so the Army boys kicked off again."

"I took the ball on the five-yard line and again went all the way for a touchdown that counted. Each time, I straight-armed one Army defensive back and knocked him out. But each time he got up, and I'm glad he did. That halfback was Dwight "Ike" Eisenhower."

The record books show that General Eisenhower played in that game, but he says he doesn't recall facing the greatest athlete of them all.

The inevitable letdown followed the Army game, and Pennsylvania measured the Indians 34-26 for the only setback of the season, handed Pop Warner's boys. Springfield scored 24 points against, although Thorpe himself racked up 30 for a 30-24 victory. They closed out the season by blanking Brown 32-0, with Jim scoring three touchdowns.

"That game is kind of foggy," said Jim. "The AAU was starting all that talk against me at that time. We got a little careless and lost to Penn, too. I guess I did okay against Brown, but I can't remember much about it. "

That was a typical Thorpe understatement. All he did was to sprint 50 yards or more for each of two touchdowns. Then, in the last minute of play, he rifled a 25-yard pass to Wheelock and followed up by bullying through the Brown line for a standing-up touchdown.

What a glorious way to close out a college football career.

Shortly afterwards came the disclosure that he had played summer baseball for $60 a month, and the AAU ruling making him a professional.

Buried in the battered scrapbook, which has no continuity or identification of many of the stories lauding Thorpe, are two little clippings that best tell the end of Jim's amateur days.

One apparently was written sometime after the Olympic games, probably while Thorpe was dominating the 1912 gridiron; the other was written shortly after he had been declared a professional.

The first reads:

"Two of the greatest athletic trophies in the world arrived at Carlisle and are now being exhibited. They are the massive bronze bust, of heroic size, in the likeness of King Gustav V of Sweden and the gift of that monarch, and a silver replica of a Norse Viking ship, gem studded, and presented by the Czar of Russia to James Thorpe, a Carlisle Indian School student, respectively, for his winning the pentathlon and decathlon in the Olympic games. Thorpe has been hailed as the greatest athlete of all time. The emperor of Russia's gift is two feet long by 18 inches high and weighs more than 30 pounds."

The other reads:

"On the American line steamship, the New York sailed today, the two big trophies won by Jim Thorpe at the Olympic games. They are en route in care of Davies, Turner, & Co. to Kristian Hellstrom, secretary of the Swedish Olympic committee."

"The bronze statue of King Gustav of Sweden and the silver Viking ship, which were presented for the pentathlon and decathlon at the last Olympic games, were received at the office of James E Sullivan, secretary of the Amateur Athletic Union, yesterday. No time was lost in transferring these trophies to the proper parties."

"Thorpe also returned to the A.A.U. his medal for the all-round championship, which he won on Labor Day, and which now reverts to J Bredemus, formerly of Princeton University."

Chapter Nine

His college playing days over, Thorpe started out for the first time to capitalize on his athletic ability. And with Warner as his financial advisor, Jim began sorting through his various offers.

Professional football as we know it today had not yet come into being. There was no money to speak of in being a professional runner, and Jim wasn't particularly keen about speech-making.

That left baseball, and there were plenty of offers from major league clubs—no less than five of them. Cincinnati and the St. Louis Cardinals offered Jim $4,000 to sign. The previous summer, Thorpe told Barney Dreyfuss, owner of the Pittsburgh Pirates, that if he ever went into professional baseball, he would sign with the Pirates. But Dreyfuss insisted that Thorpe first prove himself as a major league player.

So, when John J. McGraw, fiery leader of the New York Giants, offered Thorpe $4,500 plus $500 expense money, Dreyfuss stepped out of the bartering for the Indian's services.

The story goes that McGraw, who never had seen Jim play baseball, phoned Warner and said off-handedly:

"I hear you have a fair-looking boy down there."

Well aware that the McGraw was trying to knock down the price, Warner retorted:

"Fair? Just the world's best in anything, that's all. The big-league clubs are all after him."

At the signing, McGraw was said to have remarked skeptically that he hoped he had something good. Thorpe told McGraw he could pitch and play the outfield, but wasn't sure how he would go in the big time.

The question arose whether Thorpe was a free agent or whether he still belonged to the Fayetteville club. Secretary Farrell of the National Association cleared that matter up by ruling that Thorpe was a free agent since the league in which he played had been out of existence for several years.

Actually, McGraw needed Thorpe like a carpenter needs a sore thumb, but the Giant manager figured he had a drawing card. The Giants had won the National League pennant in 1911 and 1912 and went on to win again in 1913 with a team that included Fred Snodgrass, Rube Marquard, Josh DeVore, Larry Doyle, Fred Merkle, Chief Myers, Jeff Tesreau, and Christy Mathewson.

McGraw is reported to have said:

"If Thorpe only hits in batting practice, he'll be a big draw."

But Jim and McGraw, the martinet, never did hit it off. McGraw insisted on hustling in practice and attempted to impose strict training rules –two things that didn't fit into Thorpe's makeup.

It wasn't long before Jim found a few drinking spots where he thought he could have his beer and be safe from prying eyes, and it wasn't long before the manager's detectives found him out.

"No Indian knows how to drink," McGraw scolded his protégé.

Jim came back with the now classic retort.

"What about the Irish?"

McGraw boiled over, but Thorpe, with a grin, replied:

"I'm part Irish myself."

That was one of many bitter clashes between them. Thorpe could see no point in constant practice sessions. He could throw with any of these big leaguers, cover as much territory, and outrun them on the bases. Why practice?

Jim found more fun wrestling with bulky Jeff Tesreau, the pitcher, and smacking fungoes over the fence.

"One day, Tesreau bet me I could throw him down," Jim recalls. "So, I did, sort of wrenching his shoulder. Anyway, he couldn't pitch when his turn came around. McGraw had a fit."

Jim also tells the story of one season when he started in right field and hit .600 or better for the first six or seven games against the great Grover Cleveland Alexander. He broke up one game with a tremendous triple off the fence.

A few days later, McGraw benched him.

"I'm giving Red Murray a try in the field," he announced. Intimating that he wasn't satisfied with Jim's performance.

Jim's anger smoldered as he sat on the bench, for if there was one thing he hated, it was riding the boards. Finally, the Giants were desperately in need of a hit. McGraw called on Thorpe to bat for Murray.

As Jim picked up a bat, he said loudly:

"Why not let Murray hit? He can do a helluva lot better than Jim." McGraw was livid as Thorpe went to bat.

To this day, Jim gets a kick out of telling how he got even with McGraw.

"I took three fast cuts without looking—missing 'em a mile—and came back and sat down. I saw McGraw glaring at me. So, I said to him, "See, I told you Murray could do better."

At that, says Jim, McGraw leaped up as if shot and yelled:

"You lousy blank blank Indian! You'll never make a monkey out of me again. You're all through with this club."

And through Thorpe was with the Giants.

Thorpe has blamed McGraw for his failure to make a better showing and for spreading a false rumor that the Indian couldn't hit a curveball. But despite their differences, Thorpe still calls the Giants his team and McGraw his manager.

McGraw never used Thorpe in more than 58 games in one season, including pinch-hitting appearances. Such infrequent opportunities to hit didn't help Jim improve his "lifetime" major league batting average of .252. But the "Little Napoleon" kept bringing Thorpe back to the Giants year after year for five seasons, and he paid him as much as $7,500 a year—a big salary in those days.

After two notably unsuccessful seasons, Jim was farmed out to Jersey City and Harrisburg in 1915 and to Milwaukee in 1916. Although his hitting improved at the start of the 1917 season, he was sold to Cincinnati on a conditional deal that later was described as a "loan" to Mathewson, then manage of the Reds.

While at Cincinnati, Jim was instrumental in beating the Giants three times, almost knocking them out of the pennant. He also played an important role in one of the most memorable of all baseball games, the double no-hit pitching duel between Fred Toney of Cincinnati and Jim (Hippo) Vaughn of the Chicago Cubs.

These two fine pitchers battled through nine innings with neither allowing a hit, the only such contest in major league baseball. In the 10[th,] Larry Kopf singled and reached third on an error. Thorpe then beat out an infield hit to score Kopf and break up the ball game.

Cincinnati returned Thorpe to the Giants in August, in time for him to make his one brief appearance in a World Series. He hit .247 in 77 games that season.

In 1919, Thorpe was traded to the Boston Braves, where he batted .327—an average good enough to have won the league championship if he had played often enough. He appeared in 62 games, and Ed Roush of Cincinnati won the league battle title with .321 for 133 games.

The McGraw grapevine was operating, and Jim got a chilly reception from Manager George Stallings of the Braves. But after he had hit safely seven straight times as a pinch swinger, the fans began to yell for Old Jim, and Stallings was forced to play him more often.

But once more, his irresponsible nature and deep attachment to Rabbit Maranville, fun-loving shortstop, put Thorpe on the skids. They dropped water bags out of hotel windows on pedestrians. Jim climbed trees by moonlight and imitated a bobcat, yowling back and forth with Rabbit until the police arrived. It was all in the spirit of fun, but Stallings didn't appreciate it.

And so, a tour of the minors started and lasted until 1928. He must have learned something about hitting a curve ball, for in two seasons with Akron, Ohio, of the International League, he hit .360 and drove the ball at a .358 clip for Toledo in the American Association.

Grief rode Jim's wide shoulders while he was still with the Giants, yet he never used it as an excuse for being fired by McGraw and Stallings.

In 1913, shortly after joining the Giants, he married Iva Miller, who had attended Carlisle with him. Iva was not an Indian. She had enrolled at the Indian school through the efforts of her sister, a teacher at Chilocco Indian Institute in Oklahoma.

It was a happy marriage. Three daughters, Gale, Charlotte, and Frances, and a son, James Jr., were born to them. Jim idolized the boy. He lived for the day when he would see the sturdy youngster on the athletic field following in the footsteps of his father.

While on the road with the ball club, Jim's thoughts were only of the boy that bore his name. In New York, he couldn't get home fast enough after a ball game.

One day late in the 1918 season, Jim returned home from a game at the Polo Grounds to find his son feverish and fretful. Jim received permission to leave the team and, with his wife and son, returned to their Yale, Oklahoma home, with the boy sick all the way. On arrival, the family doctor was called, and Polio was the diagnosis.

There were no iron lungs or modern-day weapons with which to combat this dreaded disease in those days, and it took the life of the four and one-half year old boy—the boy into whom Jim had put his heart, the boy that he loved and worshipped in his quiet way as only an Indian can.

The death of Jim Thorpe's firstborn son crushed him. Nothing else mattered. Dazed and stumbling, Jim stood by while his heart's pride was lowered into the grave at Cushing, Oklahoma.

Just as he couldn't understand and never has why his Olympic trophies were taken from him, neither could Jim understand why the thing he loved most had been removed from his presence. It was almost more than the big Indian could stand, but friends never knew the grief that he buried inside himself.

Not knowing or caring, Jim found a place to drink and drink he did into a state of complete oblivion.

The road back to straight thinking was long. To be robbed of this precious possession was almost more than Jim could bear. It was a blow from which it took years to recover, but to his teammates and friends, there was never an inkling of his sorrow.

Perhaps it was some of that inward feeling coming out when he struck out as a pinch hitter for Murray the next year and was sold to the Braves. Yet he was a big enough man to come back and have his greatest year in major league baseball.

Four years later, he and Iva were divorced. Jim never said so, but friends who knew the inside story of Jim's grief said the loss of his son was the beginning of the end between the two. Iva was good for Jim, but in those days, hiding his grief, the big Indian wanted only to be alone. It was something he couldn't figure out, and it took him years to do it.

One of the highlights of Thorpe's major league baseball career was the trip around the world made by the New York Giants and Chicago White Sox after the close of the 1913 season.

And everywhere Jim went, he was the chief attraction for the sports fans; the world had never heard of his great feats at Stockholm less than two years before. The teams played in England, France, Japan, China, and several other countries.

One experience of the world tour that Jim will not forget happened in Paris. He doesn't relate it very often, for it is a story about himself.

Jim and another Giant player were sitting in a Paris Cafe, sipping wine. The other player left a few minutes later. He heard two women yell, "Any Americans here, please help."

Jim rushed over to the broad staircase and saw several French girls throwing wine on the American women. The big Indian didn't know the Americans, nor had he seen them since. But he bounced down the stairs, put a protective arm around the American woman, and led them to safety.

Word got around prior to the 1932 Olympics that the greatest athlete of them all wouldn't be present because he didn't have the price of a ticket.

Jim later said he wasn't that broke.

"I had the money but needed it for food and clothing for the family."

Jim then found he had thousands of friends—friends that he had never seen. Everybody who was nobody offered Jim a ticket. And he ended up with an honored seat in the presidential box as the guest of Vice President Charles Curtis of the United States—himself a part Indian.

And no matter how the bigwigs of the Amateur Athletic Union felt, 150,000 people gave Jim a standing ovation when he arrived at the Olympic stadium.

Six years later, Jim showed there was fire left in the big-shouldered body whenever a ball was kicked or a base hit rang out. On a movie set in 1938 during the Knute Rockne gridiron picture filming, Jim wandered by in tailfeathers, war paint, and moccasins. He was invited to match kicks with a group of college stars.

Some of them laughed at the funny old character, not knowing it was James Francis Thorpe, but they choked a moment later when he boomed a punt 15 yards past their best mark–a good 80 yards on the fly.

Along came the Second World War, and Jim tried to get into the armed services but was turned down because of his age. Finally, he signed as a ship's carpenter on an ammunition ship sailing out of San Pedro, California, for Calcutta.

"Me as a carpenter," Jim now laughs as he recalls the trip. "Old Jim, who can't even drive a nail straight."

Although Jim disappeared somewhat from the public eye, he was not forgotten.

A unit of Marines aboard an LST took an informal poll on the greatest athlete of all time prior to the invasion of Guam. Thorpe won hands down.

Though the Indian great was in his heyday long before most of the Marines were born, they had no doubts regarding his ability. One put it this way:

"If Jim was half as good as my dad said he was, he would be able to jump from our LST over the reef to Guam. He'd pick up a bushel of hand grenades and throw them like a football for 80 or 90 yards. If any pillboxes barred his path, he would vault over them. And whatever Japs he could find, he would dropkick into the ocean."

When times got tough, he would don the old war bonnet and do as many as four lecture shows a week. He still was far from a polished speaker, but the public liked his home-spun yarns, and as they cheered, Jim smiled.

There were times he regretted he had sold his farm in Oklahoma years before, for oil had been discovered in the Sac and Fox country. But with an Indian's stolid philosophy, he took it in stride.

Friends tried to get him a position in the Athletic department at the University of Oklahoma, but the idea never materialized.

Hopes that he could return to his native state came when Jim was employed as a guard at the Ford Plant in River Rouge, Michigan. There, he suffered a heart attack that threatened to cut short his life.

And again, we turned to the scrapbook—an old tailor's book filled with clippings and pictures without a thought of continuity.

There they are—stories of Jim Thorpe's appearances before civic and boys' clubs, relating his athletic experiences and calling on aid for his fellow redmen; stories of the Oklahoma legislature and other groups laying campaigns to get Thorpe's medals returned; picture of his daughter, Grace kicking a football while a member of the WAC; accounts of his teaching of clean living to boys and girls.

They are stories of Jim Thorpe living and reliving his heyday—stories that will make better men and women out of American boys and girls.

The world's greatest athlete is years past his athletic days, but he likes nothing better than to instill that spirit to win into the hearts and minds of modern-day youth, and he looks with pride on his own family –four boys and three daughters.

Richard and Jack are attending an Indian school in Oregon. Carl Phillip is a member of Uncle Sam's Army, and William is out in the business world.

Of his three daughters, all by his first wife, two, Mrs. Gail McShane and Mrs. Charlotte Kohler, live in Chicago. The other Mrs. Grace Sealey is the wife of a U.S. Army Officer stationed in Japan.

In some respects, Jim never will grow old. Were it not for his third wife, the former Patricia Gladys Askew of Louisville, Ky., when he married in 1945, he still probably wouldn't have a penny, for he has never learned to say 'No' to anybody in need.

The greatest single thing that brought Jim back into the public's eye was the Associated Press poll that voted him the greatest athlete and the foremost football player of the last 50 years.

And Mrs. Thorpe, as Jim's manager, was quick to seize the opportunity. Immediately, his services became in more and more demand as a speaker manager of other sports figures and exhibitions of kicking in football.

Warner Bros. put into production a long-dormant story depicting the life of the big Indian, and as the money rolled in, it went into the bank.

There will be no bad breaks for Jim Thorpe. He is en route back to the top financially, and his many friends are glad to see him get there.

The kids of future generations will hear of him with wonder, awe, and fascination. They might not know he was the embodiment of this country's treatment of the vanishing Indian, that he was underpaid, exploited, stripped of his rightfully earned medals, and his pride.

They may not even know exactly his records, but they'll know that JAMES FRANCIS THORPE WAS THE GREATEST ATHLETE THAT EVER LIVED – a man worthy of patterning their lives after him.

The End

Jim Thorpe Interviews 1940-1950

Touchdown Club Interview, Sept 13, 1951

Well, tonight, sports fans, our guest is one of the world's most famous sports figures. He's regarded as the greatest athlete of all time. He was the one-man Olympic team of the 1912 Olympics over in Stockholm, Sweden. And this being the Olympic year, it's very fitting indeed that we have with us tonight the noted Sac and Fox Indian, Big Jim Thorpe.

Rad: Good evening, Jim. It's a privilege and a pleasure to have you with us.

Jim: Hello, Rad. It's nice being here.

Rad: Well, first off, I'd like to go over your background so that some of our younger listeners will get an idea of what you did in the way of sports. Where did you go to school, Jim?

Jim: I went to Carlisle Indian School at Carlisle, Pennsylvania.

Rad: And what sports did you take part in?

Jim: I went out for all of them, especially track.

Rad: Especially track. Let me ask you, what sports were the kids playing out there in Oklahoma, where you were born, back in 1900?

Jim: Well, they were playing prairie baseball, as I call it, and out in the fields, why-there would be teams chewed up, and that was a baseball game that I called Prairie Baseball.

Rad: Was that the equivalent to what you call sandlot baseball?

Jim: Yes, it is.

Jim: It's the same as sandlot baseball.

Rad: What other sports were the kids interested in then?

Jim: Well, they were interested in basketball and football, but they had no track because, well, it was the day when track was a passing idea.

Rad: They had no track.

Rad: Well, how did you happen to become interested in track then, Jim?

Jim: Well, at Carlisle, when I entered Carlisle, I went out for track, and Pop Warner happened to notice me jumping over the high bar at five feet seven or eight inches, where the rest of members couldn't do it. So, I went down to practice baseball down the lower field, and Pop came down and wanted to know why I wouldn't go out for track. And he said, Well, you might have to coach someday, and if you do, you must know something about track. So, I said, well, I thought that coaching would be a good vocation, and I'd come out the next day. So, I went out the next day and started out doing everything because I wanted to become a coach, so I became the all-round athlete of the world.

Rad: Well, getting back to that track that you mentioned a moment ago, that five feet seven and a half jump, you told me a little while ago that you were in baseball uniform when that happened.

Jim: Well, I had a pair of overhauls on and a hickory shirt and a baseball cap and a pair of gymnasium shoes I picked up in the gym that belonged to someone, I guess.

Rad: I guess you topped the bar five seven and a half.

Rad: Where'd you go to college?

Jim: Didn't go to college? I went to Carlisle. Carlisle was an academic school.

Rad: That went right on through the college years.

Rad: Tell me sort of a human-interest story, that track meet between Lafayette and Carlisle, that one-man team story. Will you narrate that?

Jim: Well, it was against Lafayette and Lehigh, and the Carlisle team had about 10 members on it. So, Pop wondered when he got off the train. The coach asked Pop, he says, "Well, where's your track team?" Lafayette and Lehigh had about 60 men each out on the field. And Pop said, "Well, let's get over with the track meet. "I must catch a train to get back home." So, Carlisle won the meet.

Rad: How many events were you in that meet?

Jim: I was in about eight or nine events.

Rad: Remember how many you won out of them?

Jim: I won seven out of the eight or nine and ran second in the other two.

Rad: How old were you then, Jim?

Jim: I was around about 23 or 4.

Rad: Well, then, in 1912, you, of course, reached your greatest heights as a member of the United States Olympic team.

Rad: What events did you win?

Jim: I won the decathlon and the pentathlon.

Rad: The pentathlon is winning five events.

Jim: Yeah, five events, and the decathlon is ten.

Rad: Has any man in sports ever done that before or since?

Jim: No, they haven't.

Jim: I've been the only one to win both events.

Rad: Were you awarded any special medals for that achievement?

Jim: Well, yes.

Jim: I was awarded the Viking ship, who presented at the by the King of Sweden, and there was a bust of the King of Sweden presented by the Czar of Russia.

Rad: Right there in the Olympic Stadium.

Jim: Right.

Rad: And now we come to one of the sport's greatest tragedies.

Rad: When you returned to the United States, you were called a professional after that 1912 Olympic meet.

Rad: Why was that, Jim?

Jim: Well, I played baseball down on North Carolina, North Carolina Eastern League, and it was, well, I received expense money on my vacation time. So, I figured that I didn't play professional ball on account of the money that was in it, but I had money of my own.

Rad: You had no idea that you were.

Jim: I had no idea that I was unversed in the amateur athletic rules.

Rad: You were probably.

Jim: I didn't think I was doing anything wrong.

Rad: No, had you known, you would never have gone into the Olympics as a contestant.

Rad: Well, what happened to those Olympic Awards now, the Viking ship and the bust of the King of Sweden??

Jim: Well, they were taken from me, and...

Rad: After you got back to the States?

Jim: They were on display at Luzerne, Switzerland, at the present time.

Rad: They've been there ever since?

Jim: They've been there ever since, and I hope to get them back.

Rad: What steps have you taken to get those trophies back, Jim?

Jim: Well, there's some people out of Oklahoma City, and the Senate are trying, and well, Brundage is the man that could do that.

Rad: Isn't he Brundage is the man could recommend these trophies to be returned if he would only do it.

Rad: Do you think he will, Jim?

Jim: Just between I think I think he's good enough sport to do it because I think he's going to leave the presidency of the National Junior Olympics, or I mean the AAU, and I think that he would figure in returning these trophies to me.

Rad: So, for 36 years, you've wanted those trophies, and they've been over there in Switzerland, that's right? I understand that the runner-up in the pentathlon refused to accept the medals after they were taken away from you, and he sent you a letter.

Jim: Yes, that's right. He wrote to me that I had won, and they didn't, and they didn't want to accept the medals.

Rad: That's good sportsmanship, too.

Rad: Well, after this, you turned professional, didn't you, Jim?

Jim: Yes, I did.

Rad: Well, let's take one sport at a time.

Rad: Where did you play baseball?

Jim: I played baseball with the New York Giants and the Cincinnati Reds, and Boston Braves in the National League.

Jim: My batting average is around 320.

Rad: That's good in any league.

Rad: Where did you play football, Jim?

Jim: I played football with the Canton Bulldogs, Rock Island Independents, and, well, with the two or three other clubs, Portsmouth Spartans and the Cardinals.

Rad: I understand you played against General Eisenhower and General Patton before they were generals.

Jim: Yes, that's right, at West Point.

Jim: The Carlisle Indian's played a game up there in 1911, I think it was, and the score was 27 to 6. And I made most of the points.

Jim: Incidentally, there's a thought that I'd like to bring over to you, Rad, and that is this, that there's thrills in all football games. And the thrill to me in that game was that there was a ball kicked to me, and I took it back on my goal and ran through the army team for a touchdown.

Jim: Incidentally, there was a penalty called incident, and it kicked me again, and I ran back through the team for another.

Rad: You did it all over again. I understand, Jim, that you're in New York this week to complete plans for the filming of your life story.

Rad: How's it going?

Jim: Well, there's several producers who want to make the story.

Jim: Mrs. Thorpe is doing the negotiating.

Rad: And what was the biggest thrill that you ever had in sports yourself?

Jim: Well, catching a big fish was my biggest thrill in sports, but I guess—

Rad: Catching a big fish.

Jim: I guess in competitive sports, by being crowned the king of the world by the athletic--that is, I mean, being crowned the king of athletics by the king of Sweden in Stockholm's games in 1912.

Rad: Well, that certainly would be a thrill.

Rad: Jim, it's been a great pleasure to have you with us tonight, and we certainly hope to see your life story on the screen before too many moons have passed.

Jim: Thank you very much, sports fans.

Rad: Our guest tonight has been the greatest all-around athlete of all time, Jim Thorpe.

Rad: Tomorrow night's guest will be amateur heavyweight boxer Alfred Kahn.

And now, for those that may have tuned in late, here's a quick rundown of today's baseball.

In the National League, first game New York Giants 6, St. Louis Cards...

Giant Jottings, Steve Ellis interview with Jim Thorpe in 1948

Steve: Ladies and gentlemen, a special guest on Giant Jottings tonight, the greatest all-around sports performer of all time, Big Jim Thorpe.

Steve: Hello everybody, this is **Steve Ellis** on the New York Giants baseball sports show with our special guest of the evening again tonight.

Steve: And our broadcast, as you know and know well by this time, is beamed around the world via Armed Forces Radio.

Steve: Our guest this evening, the fellow we've been talking about lo these many years, one of the greatest athletes to ever wear any kind of sports uniform, and a terrific guy.

Steve: I'm referring to the former New York Giants baseball player, the All-America footballer, the great Olympic star, Big Jim Thorpe.

Steve: Jim, how are you this evening?

Jim: I'm pretty good, Steve.

Jim: How are you?

Steve: Well, I'm in pretty good condition.

Steve: And tell me this, if you don't mind, what are you doing these days?

Jim: Well, I'm looking for someone to make my life story in a picture if I can find the right setup.

Steve: That oughtn't to be too hard.

Steve: And what else are you doing?

Jim: Well, I'm working with the Chicago Parks District in Chicago, Illinois.

Steve: Well, Jim, tell me this and tell the fans this, as though some of them don't know.

Steve: What were some of the years you played baseball with our New York baseball giants?

Jim: Well, I started out in 1913 and finished in 1919.

Steve: And what position did you play?

Jim: I played the outfield in first base.

Steve: Well, who are some of the guys you've played with in those six good years?

Jim: Well, Big Jeff Tesreau, George Wilson, Odie Crandall, Red Ames, Christy Matheson, Furdy Shupp, and Rube Schauer.

Steve: To mention just a few, huh?

Jim: Yeah, well, the catching department with Chief Myers and Art Wilson.

Jim: Outfield with Georgie Burns and Robertson, and Becker.

Steve: And a guy named Thorpe.

Jim: Yes, I played the outfield.

Steve: And how you did?

Steve: Well, tell us this.

Steve: You were the Mr. Olympics of 1912.

Steve: Where were the 12 Olympic Games held?

Jim: They were held in Stockholm, Sweden.

Steve: And what were some of the events you were in, Jim?

Jim: Well, I was entered in the Decathlon and the Pentathlon.

Steve: How'd you do?

Jim: Well, I won both.

Steve: Were you the only man in sports history to win both those events?

Jim: Yes, that's right.

Steve: Uh-huh.

Steve: Well, when did you play football?

Steve: And we're dating back in your career right now,

Jim: I see that.

Jim: Well, I played with the Carlisle Indians in 1907-8, 11, and 12.

Steve: Uh-huh.

Steve: Well, you played under coach Pop Warner, didn't you?

Jim: Yes, I did.

Steve: Would you say that you made Glen S. Pop Warner famous, or did he make Jim Thorpe famous?

Jim: Well, I think it worked both ways.

Steve: I'd agree with you on that.

Steve: And I think you really gave Pop quite a start.

Steve: Well, let's see, you played football and you played baseball.

Steve: And I want to ask you this.

Steve: Any other sport or any sport you didn't play?

Jim: Well, I guess I didn't play tiller rinks or dominoes.

Steve: I guess you didn't.

Steve: Well, Jim, tell me this. Down through these 40 successful years that you've been in and associated and around sports, has sports changed much in your opinion?

Jim: Well, yes, they have, for instance, in track, they have specialties.

Jim: And in football, why they have the man in motion and the lateral passes and individual blocking.

Jim: So that changes track and changes football.

Steve: You'd say then that sports these days would become a specialized art.

Jim: Yes, because the fact that you have 30 to one of the players of today than you had when I was playing.

Jim: We were lucky to have a good substitute when I was playing.

Steve: Is that right?

Steve: I didn't realize that. In other words, you have more guys participating these days.

Jim: That's right.

Steve: Well, Jim, what is your favorite sport or sports?

Jim: Well, I love fishing and hunting, but in competitive athletics, why, I think track is the important call for our youngsters of American youth for the buildup of their health.

Steve: You've always been a great guy for the kids of America.

Steve: You'd say then that for the youngsters of our country that they ought to participate in track and field.

Jim: That's right.

Steve: Well, Jim, what do you think our chances are now that the Olympics are getting underway in the Olympic Games of 1948?

Jim: Well, I think we should win with hands down.

Steve: Why?

Jim: Well, because the athletes of today are specialists, and they specialize in certain events.

Jim: And I think we'll win, as I said, with hands down.

Steve: Well, that's true.

Steve: In other words, you think this country ought to cop the titles.

Jim: Oh, yeah, sure.

Steve: Well, Jim, you're a pretty busy guy.

Steve: Let's see. You're going to make that movie, and we'll look forward to seeing it.

Steve: And you're also, I understand, from your lovely wife doing lots of writing these days about sports, and you're busy enough to do some fishing.

Steve: Do you think you'd like me to do some management of a guy called Jim Thorpe?

Jim: Well, I think you're about 40 years too late because I've signed up with a Bernard Howard of Chicago, who is a producer and radio and television.

Steve: In other words, you've gotten yourself a real good manager.

Jim: That's right.

Steve: Well, I'm 40 years too late, and I wish I'd been around before Bernard, but is he the guy who did such a wonderful job on one of our announcing buddies,

> making him quite a famous fellow, Bob Elson?

Jim: Yes, that's right.

Steve: I thought I remember hearing that name.

Steve: Well, Jim, I want to thank you most sincerely for coming down to our New York Giants sports show this evening.

Steve: You kind of belong on this broadcast, you know that, and lots of continued success and a tremendously athletic career good night to you now, and our kindest regards to all your many many friends in the world of sporting you run into from time to time.

Jim: Thank you.

Steve: Ladies and gentlemen, our special guest tonight on giant jottings New York Giants sports show, the all-time sports performer, one of the all-time greats in the world, Big Jim Thorpe.

Steve: Well, this is Steve Ellis saying so long now 'til tomorrow night in the world of sports for another top interview.

Steve: And by the way, it'll be Leo DeRocher, the new manager of the New York Giants.

Interview at the Polo Grounds during a New York Giants game - London Olympics 1948

Al: Hiya, folks.

Al: Kind of surprised, aren't you?

Al: No baseball uniform, no tails.

Al: I feel a little lost.

Al: Well, folks, this show has a big, really has a big surprise today.

Al: I'm about to introduce you to the greatest athlete the world has ever known.

Al: And I'm speaking all around the athlete.

Al: You know, we got the Olympics going on in London now.

Al: We're talking about Olympics.

Al: I'm gonna have you meet one of the greatest Olympic winners, I would say the greatest.

Al: Well, let's bring him in right away.

Al: Jim Thorpe, the greatest athlete the world has ever known.

Al: Come in, Jim.

Al: I want you to meet my friends out there.

Al: Sit down, Jim.

Al: Let's go for a few details here.

Al: Have you been following the Olympics?

Jim: Yes, I have, Al.

Al: How do you think we're going to do?

Jim: Well, the United States should win with hands down.

Al: Fine.

Al: Well, you ought to know, you were in the Olympics once, what was it, 1912 at Stockholm, Sweden?

Al: You did a pretty good job there, by the way.

Al: How many events did you win there out there?

Jim: I won the two all-round events, the decathlon and the pentathlon.

Jim: I won 11 out of 15, not less than third in the other four.

Al: It kind of slowed up in a few, didn't you?

Al: You got quite a few medals, didn't you, Jim?

Jim: Yes, I got two trophies.

Al: And what happened to those medals and those trophies?

Jim: Well, they're Luzerne, Switzerland, on permanent display at the present time.

Al: Oh, they took them away from you, didn't they?

Jim: Yes, I turned them back to the AAU, and they returned them back to the second place, athletes, and they didn't accept them.

Al: Well, why did they take it?

Al: Why did they make you give them up?

Jim: Well, I played summer professional baseball down in Rocky Mountain, North Carolina, in Fayetteville.

Al: How much money did you get that day?

Jim: Well, I got $60 a month.

Al: A lot of money.

Jim: Expense money is all.

Al: Say, well, I'm going to get into football, Jim.

Al: You know, I know I'm going to ask you a few questions, Jim, and I don't want to embarrass you.

Al: I know you never like to talk about your great athletic prowess and your football work.

Al: But they do say, and I know it for a fact, that you're the greatest football player that ever lived.

Al: Now, Jim, you played in Carlisle with the Carlisle Indians under Pop Warner, is that right?

Jim: That's right.

Al: And you also played against Newt Rockne in professional football.

Al: Would you tell us that story about, I heard about you and Newtie, would you tell me that story?

Jim: It was a professional game played at Maslin High, and Rockne was on the Maslin Tigers, and I was on the Canton Bulldogs.

Jim: And he played left end, and I was playing left half, but consequently, I had to go around his end.

Jim: And he slipped through and tackled me for a couple of yard losses.

Jim: And I said, attaboy, Rock,

Jim: I said, "You're doing fine.

Jim: But I said, look at the people who come up here to see old Jim run.

Jim: How about letting old Jim run?

Jim: And he said, well, if you think you can get away with that, I'd like to see it.

Jim: So, the next time I carried the ball around, I hit him in the side of the head with my knee, spin it off for a 60-yard touchdown.

Jim: And on the point after touchdown, why, here comes Rock with a player under each arm, all wet down with a sponge, and I walked up and patted him on the shoulder.

Jim: Rock, you let old Jim run, didn't you?

Al: And the way I heard the story, he said, you know, when Big Jim wants to run, he runs, and boy, you used to run.

Al: Now, Jim, I think, I hope you've seen this.

Al: You know what this is, don't you?

Jim: Oh, yes, it's a great coffee.

Jim: We use it at our home.

Jim: We've been using it for years.

Al: Well, you know, the folks will agree with me when I tell you, and as you know, it's great coffee because it's delicious.

Al: I stir hot.

Al: It's all coffee, nothing but coffee, Jim.

Al: You and I keep drinking this coffee.

Al: And maybe if you just continue drinking this coffee, we might send you over there in the Olympics again.

Al: By the way, what are you planning to do now?

Jim: Well, there's a moving picture deal we're trying to get set up so that a producer will produce my life story.

Al: By the way, Jim, let's you and I go up to the Polo Grounds now and watch those New York Giants.

Al: They're going hot now and see if we can get them another winner.

Al: Well, Jim, it's been nice to see you.

Al: Goodbye and good luck to you.

Al: So long, folks.

Ernie Saunders with WCHS

Jim: I'm a little late, of course, but that couldn't be helped, I suppose.

Jim: The plane stopped in Washington, D.C. because of the weather down through here,

Jim: So, I had to take the train.

Jim: Naturally, taking the train takes a long time, and I just arrived a few minutes ago.

Jim: It's a pleasure to be here, and I'll be around tomorrow.

Jim: And if you want me to come shake hands, I'll be good to do it.

Frank: I want to thank you.

Jim, we made a regular program that was a pretty nifty program.

Frank: It made you feel good, even if you weren't there.

Frank: So, we're going to make this thing a little bit informal, and because Ernie Saunders here with WCHS is much more adept at interviewing celebrities than I am,

Frank: I wonder if you'd let him start a takeover and then we're gonna tape record this thing it's if it doesn't set me off all right

Jim: Thank you very much, Frank

Frank: And Jim could you step up a little closer please

Ernie: We're glad that you finally made it
       into town I understand this isn't your
       first visit to Charleston.

Ernie: You've been here before, haven't you?

Jim: Oh yes I've been here before with a
       traveling baseball club and also with
       a traveling basketball team

Ernie: What were you going to speak of before
       the Touchdown Club this evening?

Jim: Well, I don't know on my experiences
       in athletics, I suppose, and talk on
       the Indian question some about my
       trophies and one thing or another.

Ernie: Well, it's really too bad that the
       elements had to interfere, Jim,
       because we were all looking forward to
       your coming here.

Ernie: Jim, just how do you feel about the
       emphasizing of present-day athletics
       as compared to those of the past?

Jim: Well, in football, your platoon system
       takes over at the present time.

Jim: That's rather hard for a commentator
       like yourself to select an All-
       American, I figure, because of the
       fact that you have a defensive club
       and an offensive club with specialties
       running in and out all the time.

Jim: Whereas you have 30 to one of the ball players that they did when I was playing, I was lucky to have a good substitute.

Jim: So consequently, I had to stay in for 60 minutes of play.

Ernie: Well, Jim, wouldn't you say then that the football player of the past was a better football player than the modern-day player for the simple reason that he could do a lot more things?

Jim: Well, I don't say that he's any better, but I think he was in condition a little bit better and could stand the gaffe a little better than these fellows today because of the fact today, they'll just run in and out, as I say.

Jim: And they just go in for one play and come back out.

Jim: And that's all they've done every day's work, I suppose.

Ernie: Well, Jim, you have a reputation for being very durable.

Ernie: In all your career as a football player, as an athlete, too, did you suffer many injuries?

Jim: Well, no, I haven't suffered too much.

Jim: I had a shoulder thrown out and a rib cracked here and there, but that's about all, I guess.

Ernie: Well, you look pretty good right now.

Jim: Thank you.

Ernie: Jim, are you still in hopes of having the medals you won in the 1912 Olympics return to you?

Jim: Well, yes.

Jim: There's been a lot of publicity put out here lately because of the fact that the medals, are missing at the present time.

Jim: They were supposed to be at Luzerne Switzerland on permanent display.

Jim: But what I found out from the Associated Press is that they can't run them down now.

Jim: Someone has taken them, or they might be here in America.

Jim: I don't know.

Jim: But the Associated Press is going to try to find them.

Ernie: Well, as a matter of fact, I was reading someplace, Jim, where there's a campaign underway to maybe have those medals represented to you at the 1952 Olympics at Helsinki.

Ernie: And how would you feel about something like that?

Jim: Well, I'd appreciate it very much because the American youth, I think that, well, athletics is a standout here in this country because it builds up health and it builds up citizenry ideals and one thing or another to be able to go out and do athletics, that is the girls and the boys both.

Jim: So, I figured that they would like the medals reprieved to me.

Jim: I'd appreciate it, and I think the American youth would also.

Ernie: Well, Jim, I think all of us here in Charleston and vicinity will definitely go on record as being in agreement with you.

Ernie: We think the medal should be returned to you.

Ernie: How about a crowd, don't you agree?

Ernie: Now, Jim.

Ernie: Did the youth of our country, to say nothing of the adults think of you as, well, probably the world's all-time great athlete?

Ernie: Now, what would you advise the potential athlete of tomorrow to remember most of all?

Jim: That is, you mean to become an athlete?

Ernie: That's right, Jim.

Jim: Well, I'd suggest that you exercise in the open and get plenty of good rest and plenty of good sleep, and like God wanted us to be.

Ernie: Jim you know I might explain to our radio audience as well as the people here this is strictly unrehearsed interview Jim just came in it was a little late the elements held him back he had to catch a train in Washington, he hasn't seen any of the questions we've been asking him and I think he's doing a great job of answering them ad-lib.

Ernie: Well Jim, in all your years in sports what stands out as your greatest thrill well?

Jim: I don't know, I enjoyed fishing a whole lot and hunting.

Jim: But I suppose you mean in athletics.

Ernie: That's right, Jim.

Jim: Well-being crowned the greatest athlete of the world by the King of

Sweden, I think, was one of my great moments in my life.

Ernie: Well, I should imagine that would stand out.

Ernie: Anything else?

Ernie: I mean, any particular event, perhaps at the time you kicked five field goals against Harvard, would that stand out?

Jim: Well, yes, in football, playing against the Army one year when Carlisle played, we scored 27 to 6, and I scored 22 points.

Jim: There was a ball kicked to me back on my goal line and I ran through the Army for a touchdown.

Jim: But there was a penalty called, so the ball had to be kicked over.

Jim: Incidentally, it was kicked to me again and I took it right back through for another touchdown.

Ernie: Jim, all of us here in Charleston are well aware of the fact that you're much better looking than Burt Lancaster, who played you in the movie Jim Thorpe: All-American.

Ernie: Do you think that Burt did a pretty good job of impersonating you?

Jim: Yes, I did.

Jim: I thought he did a very good job, and
         he's quite an athlete on his own
         account because he's an acrobat and
         circus stunts and one thing or
         another, so he didn't know too much
         about football, though.

Jim: And in fact, we had to show him a whole
         lot, he came through very nicely and
         done a great deal, I think, for the
         picture.

Ernie: Well, that picture has certainly been
         a hit.

Ernie: I know it did turn away business here
         in Charleston, Jim.

Ernie: And another thing we want to ask you,
         too, what do you plan to do after you
         leave Charleston?

Ernie: I understand you're making all kinds of
         appearances.

Ernie: Where do you go from here?

Jim: Well, I think I'll spend my Christmas
         down in Memphis, Tennessee for the
         holidays, or I might go to New Orleans
         to the New Year's Orange Bowl game
         there.

Jim: I've been invited down there, so I may
         go there.

Ernie: All right, Jim, now we're going to turn
         off our recording here.

Ernie: That's all the time we have for On the
Air, but we're going to continue this
interview here at the Assembly Hall.

Appendix

GLENN S. WARNER
Palo Alto, Calif.

Having been Jim Thorpe's coach from the time he started to develop his world famous athletic career until he finished his course at the Carlisle Indian School I naturally came to know him very well.

During those years at Carlisle Jim developed from a green country kid into the most outstanding athlete in the whole world. He not only won the Olympic all around ten events and five event Track and field championship and the American all around championship, breaking all records, but he also became the greatest football player of his time and became a major league base ball player. Carlisle did not promote basket ball but I am sure Jim would have achieved national prominence in that sport if he had engaged in it.

All through Jim's athletic career he was an easy going care free chap. He lived in the present and never seemed to think seriously about his future. He was honest and frank and a good sportsman. There was no sham or guile in his makeup — That explains why he

used his real name when he spent a
vacation playing base ball in a small
Carolina league, composed mostly of
northern and New England college boys
who played under assumed names
to preserve their amateur standing.

This honesty eventually lost him
his amateur standing and his
Olympic trophies and medals

Jim Thorpe has been a care free
and the same lovable character ever
since his Carlisle days. He has taken
things easy and made many friends
but never has cashed in to any great
extent upon his remarkable athletic
ability and world wide reputation as
he would have been able to do if he had
taken life and especially his future
welfare more seriously.

Glenn S. Warner

Dear Robertson,
            You can condense or change
or add to the above in any way you like
providing I am quoted in no way of
criticism. I would like to have a copy of the
book when ready. P.J.

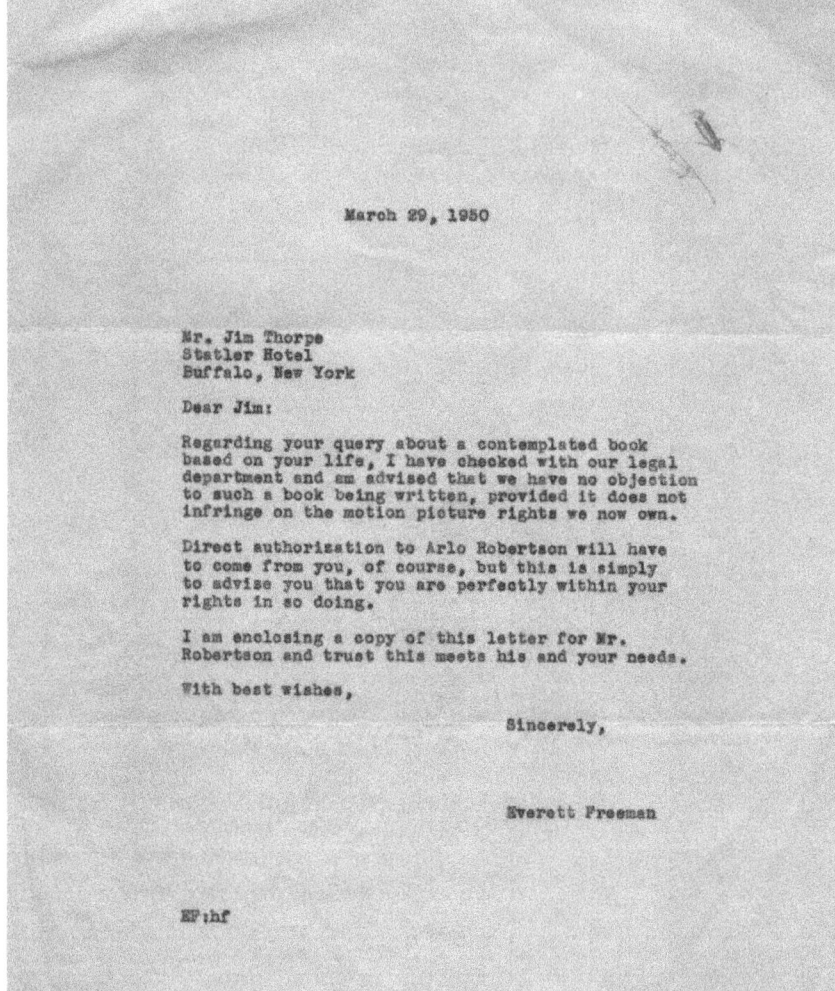

March 29, 1950

Mr. Jim Thorpe
Statler Hotel
Buffalo, New York

Dear Jim:

Regarding your query about a contemplated book
based on your life, I have checked with our legal
department and am advised that we have no objection
to such a book being written, provided it does not
infringe on the motion picture rights we now own.

Direct authorization to Arlo Robertson will have
to come from you, of course, but this is simply
to advise you that you are perfectly within your
rights in so doing.

I am enclosing a copy of this letter for Mr.
Robertson and trust this meets his and your needs.

With best wishes,

Sincerely,

Everett Freeman

EF:hf

EXECUTIVE OFFICES
321 WEST 44th STREET
NEW YORK

TELEPHONE
HOLLYWOOD 9-1251

PICTURES, INC.
WEST COAST STUDIOS
BURBANK, CALIFORNIA

March 29, 1950

Mr. Jim Thorpe
Statler Hotel
Buffalo, New York

Dear Jim:

Regarding your query about a contemplated book
based on your life, I have checked with our legal
department and am advised that we have no objection
to such a book being written, provided it does not
infringe on the motion picture rights we now own.

Direct authorization to Arlo Robertson will have
to come from you, of course, but this is simply
to advise you that you are perfectly within your
rights in so doing.

I am enclosing a copy of this letter for Mr.
Robertson and trust this meets his and your needs.

With best wishes,

Sincerely,

Everett Freeman

EF:hf

107

AIR MAIL

THE ASSOCIATED PRESS AB
KLARA S. KYRKOGATA 18
STOCKHOLM, SWEDEN

April 14, 1950

Mr. Orlo Robertson,
The Associated Press,
Philadelphia

Dear Mr. Robertson,

I have your letter of April 4 with a request
for a letter signed by King Gustav V.

I would have been happy to help you with this.
King Gustav, however, is at present staying, as a
convalescent after a serious illness, at Nice, France.
He will return to Stockholm in the last week of May or,
maybe, even later.

If this is not too late for you please send me
a line to that effect. I will then do my very best to
obtain the requested letter. I would stress, though,
that the King is a very old and frail man, being 93 years
of age. He might not remember Jim Thorpe after such a
long time.

Sincerely yours,

FOLKE PALM,
CHIEF OF BUREAU

THE ASSOCIATED PRESS
BULLETIN BUILDING
PHILADELPHIA 5, PA.

July 20, 1950

Dear Patricia:

Received your letter from Las Vegas today and sure sorry to hear that you have been going through so much hell but also glad to hear that you are on the mend.

That angle of Warner brothers looking over the manuscript sounds interesting. I'll leave it to you to drive a right bargain. I am sending under separate cover chapters covering Jim's Olympic performances and his 1912 year in football.

Also will have underway to you by Saturday his career in major league baseball and perhaps the chapter or two on pro football. The latter, for the most part, is a xxxxxxx series of stories which I got from Jim and many other sources.

Have been working odd hours the last few weeks so got behind my schedule on the writing but will pick it rapidly. As I told you in the last letter I have some more information that will need go in the part you now have. Also the description of the 1911 Harvard football game. When writing it I had the impression it was played in 1912 but closer check of Jim's scrap books find that I was wrong.

So if Warners should use any of that they should have some of the dope on that game, because it was one of Jim's outstanding performances. The part being sent under separate cover now ix has been signed by a notary but there is some doubt if I can the section that will be mailed saturday or sunday notarized since offices will be closed.

I don't know what scrip Warners used for putting together the movie but I bet there is a lot in this book that they never knew about.

Incidentally, was talking with Bob Kelly, the New York publisher, the other day and he is still interested in publishing the book. It is the Kelly publishing co., 309 Lafayette. Perhaps Warners might want to publish it and tie it in with the picture if they use the material.

Will be waiting to hear from you and best of luck on your return to health and my regards to James Francis.

Sincerely,

Carlo Robertson

111

THE ASSOCIATED PRESS
BULLETIN BUILDING
PHILADELPHIA 5, PA.

Aug. 18, 1950

Dear Patricia:

Enclosed is the part of the manuscript you are missing. Right after this goes the part of the death of Jim's first boy. But in looking over the movie script I find the boy became ill after the 1919 Baseball season while Jim was playing football. Is that correct?

The notes you gave me said he came home from a baseball game at the Polo Grounds and found the boy ill. If that it is wrong the story will need revising. There also are some facts in the script about his return to the football team which I did n o t know.

Knowing that movies do n o t always follow true to life I suggest you let me know and I'll improve on that part of the book greatly.

I am returning the movie script under separate cover as want to read it over carefully again and take some notes. And incidentally when the postman delivered it I thought the Thorpes must be broke. There was $1.36 postage due.

The movie sounds fine although I note they call Jim's first wife Margaret. Is that because you didn't get clearance. I always thought it was Iva Miller.

Let me know how you are coming out as soon as possible, then read the copy for any additions or deletions so it can be whipped into final shape.

Best of Regards,
Orlo Robertson

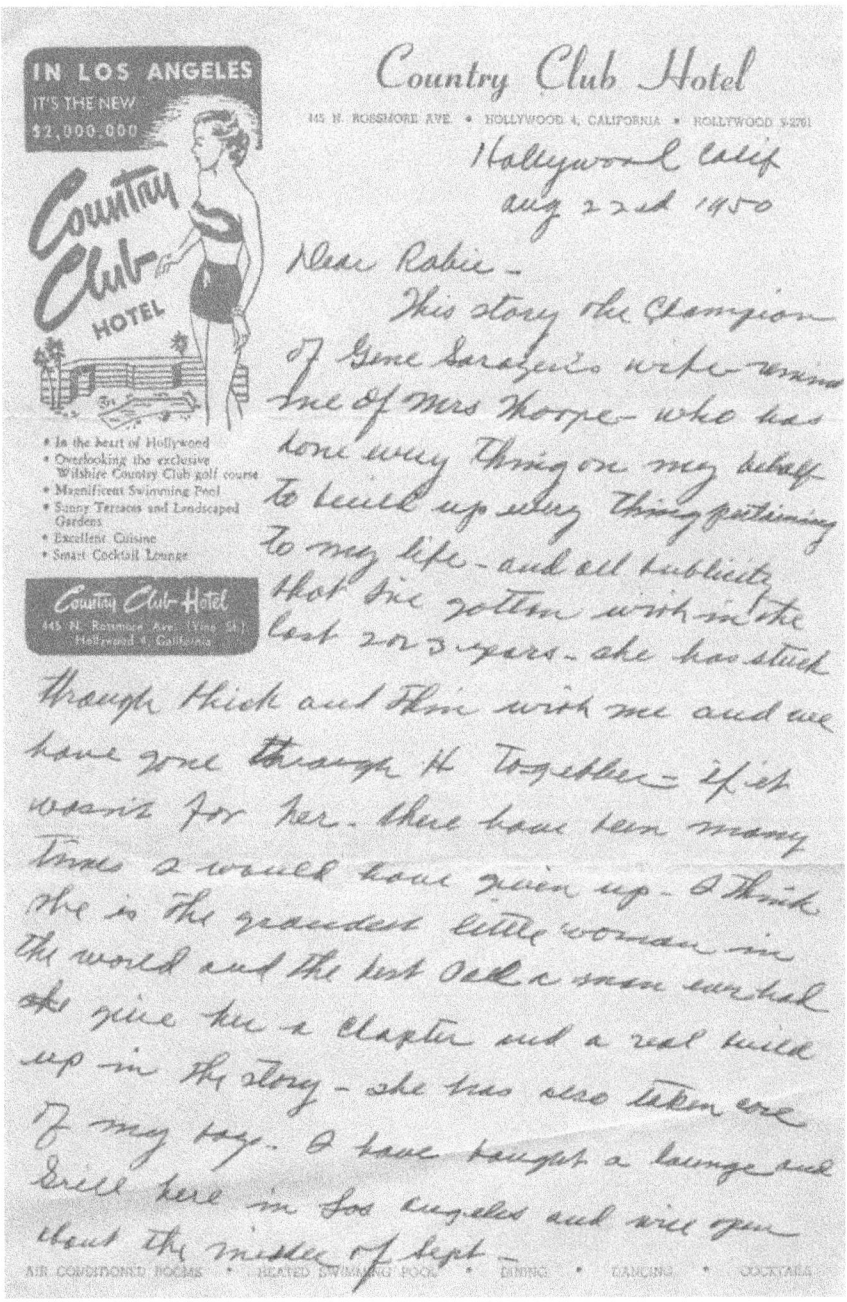

Country Club Hotel

445 N. ROSSMORE AVE. • HOLLYWOOD 4, CALIFORNIA • HOLLYWOOD 3-2761

Hollywood Calif
aug 22nd 1950

Dear Robie –

This story the Champion
of Gene Sarazen's write wrote
one of mrs thorpe – who has
done every thing on my behalf
to build up every thing pertaining
to my life – and all publicity
that she gotten with in the
last 2 or 3 years – she has stuck
through thick and thin with me and we
have gone through it together – if it
wasn't for her. there have been many
times I would have given up. I think
she is the grandest little woman in
the world and the best Oella man ever had
she gave her a chapter and a real build
up in the story – she has also taken care
of my boy – I have bought a lounge and
grill here in Los angeles and will open
about the middle of Sept –

Anita Thorpe

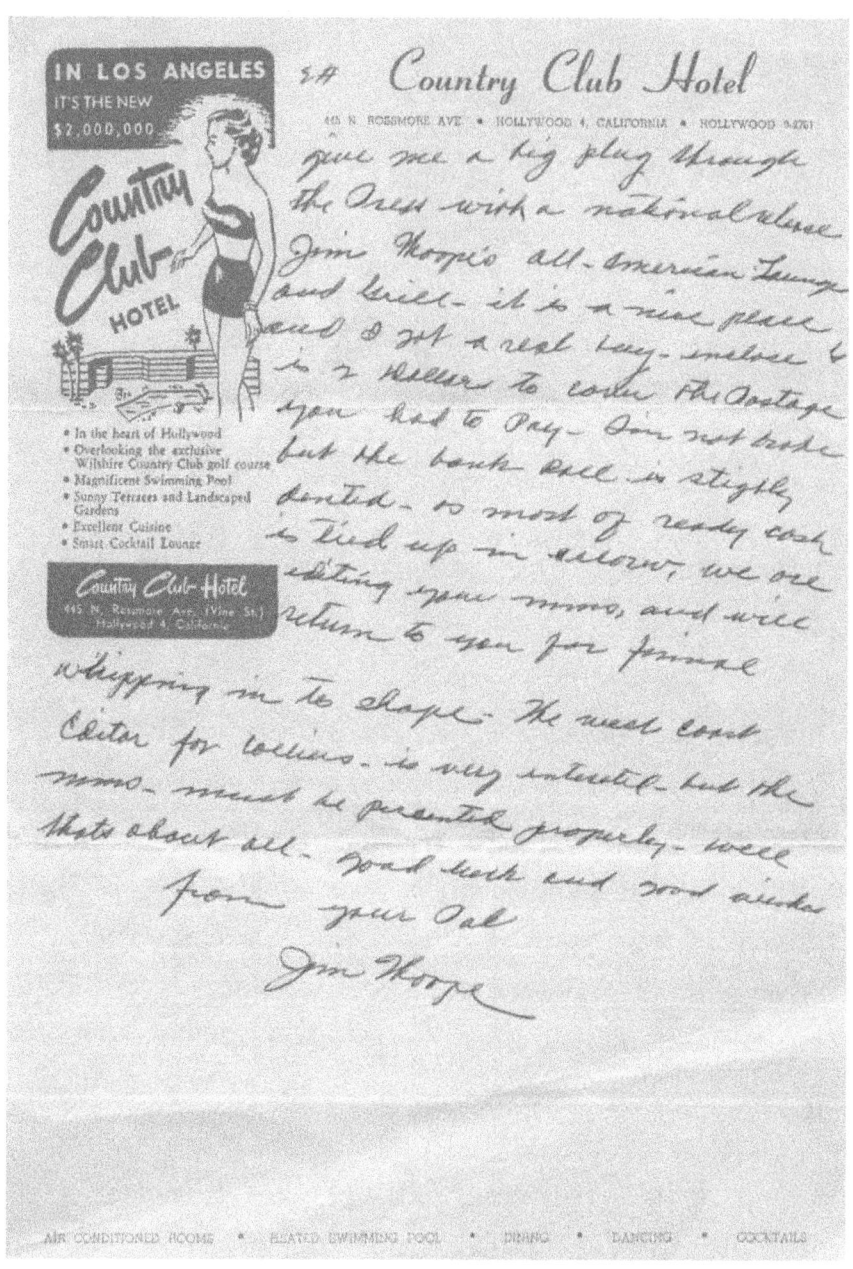

114

HOTEL *Statler* BUFFALO

March 28th, '50

Dear Robbie;

Your letter of the 22nd. I have been on the jump and am just now getting
around to answering you. I talked with E Freeman, producer of the picture
regarding your wanting to know about infringing on the rights of Warner Bro
he assured me they did not have book rights, but did not want the book out
before the picture. I asked him why h e was so determined that Jim not make
a dollar? We had it hot and heavy over long distance and I told him to get
the statement into my hands or all hell would break loose, he stated that
he would but I have not yet recieved it.

Golly theresems to be a terrible storm coming up. The wind is howling
around the corner of the hotel and it is getting very dark.Here comes the
rain and it is really beating against the windows. I obtained a terrific
rate for Jim here, sitting room bed room $5.00a day!

Had a call from Jim Clark yesterday, he wanted to know when Jim will be aval
available, so...... that deal is on. I may run over to Philly before I
leave for the coast next week, to show you the Warner Bros contract and get
Jim Clark's deal tied up. I am furious at Freeman fro holding me up on this
and he will be sorry believe me.

I have not had time to write the Paris episode but will either send it to
you or tell you about it if I come over. Jim is making Buffalo his head
quarters until the first of June. He left yesterday for Albany where his
boy wrestled last night and won, Syracuse tonight and he will be back here
before morning.

You will be able to see him in between engagements, he is to take War Cloud
all over the eastern states, and may be difficult to catch up with, but we
both will co-operate with you in every way possible. Jim has made a lot of
money during his sport carreer, close to a million, h e gave it away, un
sound investments, high living etc.

If the people in Nexonpeck will contact Ed Don George here 300 Main St, he
may let Jim go, but the price is up now Robbie $350.00 plus expenses. I
doubt if George will let him go. When Jim finishes this contract he goes to
the coast to act as technical adviser, then back to Philadelphia to Jim
Clark. I like Mr. Clark. He is a smart man, a Democrat and a C atholic. Thi
Those are my sentiments too.

I'll try to get over therebefore I leave and bet everything straightened out

Our best to you always,

Patricia G. Thorpe.

WILL YOU PLEASE GET THOSE PICTURES OF JIM IN THE DIFFERENT SPORTS TO
ME THEY ARE MOST IMPORTANT FOR A PUBLICITY PAMPLET, I HAVE AN ARTIST
STANDING BY WAITING FOR THEM. PGT

SAN BERNADINO CALIF.
APRIL 30th 1950

DEAR ROBBIE:

I AM ABOUT READY TO TKE THE VEIL. I HAVE BEEN ON MILK FOR THE PAST TWO
WEEKS AND I AM FEELING A LOT BETTER. THIS IS TO ADVISE YOU THAT JIM WILL
BE IN MANHATTAN SOMETIME THIS WEEK OR NEXT AT THE BELVEDERE HOTEL. I
WOULD SUGGEST THAT YOU KEEP CONTACTING THE HOTEL UNTIL YOU REACH HIM AND
JUMP INTO THE CITY TO HAVE YOUR TALK WITH HIM.

I HAVE NEVER HEARD FROM MR. KELLY SINCE I ARRIVED ON THE COAST. THERE ARE
PUBLISHERS OUT HERE, ASSOCIATES OF THE EASTERN PEOPLE WHOM I WILL CONTACT
IN THE NEXT TWO WEEKS. HOW IS THE BOOK PROGRESSING?

I HAVE MADE NO EFFORT TO DO ANY BUISNESS WHATEVER OTHER THAN WARNERS AND
JIM CLARK. I TALKED WITH THE LATTER TH RUSDAY AND TOLD HIM I WANT TWO
THOUSAND A WEEK FOR JIM THIS SEASON. I SHALL PROBABLY HAVE TO COME DOWN.

DO A GOOD JOB ON THE BOOK, FOR I WANT ALL THE OTHER DEALS AROUND IT. I
INTEND TO HAVE A SEQUEL TO THE PICTURE, BASED ON YOUR BOOK. JIM'S BOYS
WILL BE COMING HOME FROM SCHOOL THE 18th OF MAY, SO YOU CAN SEE I AM
GOING TO HAVE MY HANDS FULL WHAT WITH TRYING TO GET WELL ETC.

THE TROUT SEASON OPENED HERE TODAY, BUT IT IS TOO COLD TO GO FISHING. THE
SUN SHONE ABOUT TEO HOURS YESTERDAY AND I WISH I HAD STAYED IN PALM SPRINGDS
HOWEVER. AS I HAVE TO DRIVE INTO HOLLYWOOD ONCE A WEEK TO MY DOCTOR AND DENT
1ST, THIS IS ONLY SIXTY MILES AWAY, SO I THINK I SHALL REMAIN HERE UNTIL
JIM COMES TO THE COAST.

DID I TELL YOU THAT I HAVE AN ALMA TRAILER COACH, AND I AAN HOOK ON AND
MOVE WHEN I GET TIRED OF ONE PLACE. I LOVE IT. JTUST LIKE PLAYING HOUSE
AND CAMPING OUT. WHY DIDNT I THINK OF THIS BEFORE. IT IS RESTFUL, WRITE
TO ME AT THE HOLLYWOOD ADDRESS AND TELL ME HOW THINGS ARE.

I WILL WIRE YOU, IF I HAVE ANY DEFINITE DATE ABOUT WHEN JIM WILL BE IN N.Y.
HIS LETTER OF YESTERDAY JUST SAID NEXT WEEK.

BEST AE ALL GOOD WISHES TO YOU, AND LET ME HEAR FROM YOU

Cordially
Patricia Y. J.

Hollywood Calif.
June 13th 50

Dear Orlo;

Things have been a mess since I last wrote to you. I recieved the mms. but
have not been able to do anything about it. First I had a general collapse
when I returned here. Then all my upper teeth had to be removed. Then the
two youngest boys came home from school, then Jim came home. My doctor
told me to either get out from under or I would wind up in the booby hatch.

I am still very nervous and not capable of doing the things which should be
done. Jim starts the 15th at Warners. We have read the script and it stinks

Your story is very good;I have made a few corrections and havne been able t
or had time to even look at it since the first two days I had it.

I am sending the boys to summer camp the 26th. It is my hope that I may hav
a little rest and then start the ball rolling again. I think the Eagle deal
is not to be. I could not handle things while I was ill and they did not
wish to pay any money anyway. I do not understand people like that. They w
wanted Jim but when it come to putting any money on the line, well I guess
we are supposed to eat grass according to them.

I am so terribly worn out that you can consider this a courtesy letter, wh
which you should have had some time ago, and I could not fullfill my
obligation. If I can get some rest, I will get on the ball again. But there
is no use in trying to do any buisness in the set up as it now is.

The motion picture will be first shown in the Cumberland Valley according
to the producer. Tell Clark or the Eagles buisness manager that, will you
please. Penn. will be the scene of most of the action in the picture.

That is all I can tell you at this time dear boy, but after I get the boys
situatiated I hope to be able to start pushing again. It seems that when I
go down every thing stops.

So, bue for now. If you can interest a publisher, go ahead. It may be a moh
month brfore I can take hold of it from this end. There has been a good off
offer here in California for Jim to head a big rodeo. But I cant seem to
work up any enthusiam for any thing at this time.

Best of all things Orlo. Let us here from you at the Melrose address.

Patricia G. T.

Las Vegas Nevada
Sunday July 16th 1950

Dear Robbie;

I am just out of the hospital from having my gall bladder removed, hence the long silence. I am getting around a little and will try to get things whipped into shape in the next week or so.

We are trting to get a manager for Jim, It is very evident that I will be unable to caryy on. It is a damaed shame, for me to go down right when things are beginning to pop.

Came over here to get out of the dampness on the coast and believe me it is hotter than hades. 115 no shade.

Jim has dropped 32 lbs in the past two months and is still on diet and exceroise. He has been pratice kicking and doing amazingly well. It seems that when I am not on the job, everything fals to pieces.

The mms. is in Hollywood, I will be going over there in the next two weeks I am goint to try to get Warners to use it for the picture. We are making them re do the story any way. So-, please send on what you have done so far. I should like the story brought upnas car as you have time and an outline from there to present to Everett Freeman. It is possible they may use your story and that will be very good for all concerned.

Please do as I ask and get it to me at the Hollywood Melrose. I am not too strong yet, but by being careful will come out of it, I hope, Teeth ulcer, gall baldder etd, all at once relly knocked me for a loop. But thank Gid it all did not destroy my lousy stubborn disposition I will do all in mypower to put your story over. Have it notorized before you send it, in your name, that is pratically the same as a copyright and if they want your material they will have to pay for it.

Wiht best wishes to you, and I sincerely believe things will work out O K I am Cordially yours as Always,

Patricia

The picture is SUPPOSED to go in ot production the 24th of this month and be on the screens the in Oct Or Nov.
PGT

Los Angeles Calif
July 28th 1950

Dear Orlo;

Find enclosed the corrected mns. We have the script and dialogue of Jim
Thorpe All American and it is going to make a beautiful picture. The activ
at the studio is terrific and Jim has been working very hard. He goes today
on location. By this time next week things will start to move rapidly.

Freeman wishes Jim to remain on the picture for the entire time. The
premiere will be in the Cumberland Valley of Penn, and possibly be followed
up in Oklahoma before a general release is made.

Clark has really missed the boat, but I suppose it was caused mostly by my
illness. Jim can still get permission to fly to Chicago to kick off for the
Eagles if Clark will wire or call for him to come and furnish air transport
ation. Can you get that message through to him in time.

I am feeling much better and am interviewing a prospective publicity man
today at two; We have been offered a suite of rooms at the fabalous Country
Club Hotel here, and I am meeting M M Miller the owner this afternoon to
see about that. Now that I am getting back on the beam I shall be able to
sent things in motion again.

I have had neither the time nor felt well enough to press through for
publication of the book, but will get at it now.

Please forward to me, the following chapters as rapidly as you can. I
should have a copy of all chapters in my posession to submit. Jim is now
going over your story and soon as he is finished I will prepare it for returning to you.

Tmes a wasting now. It is a shame I had to get sick right at the crucial
time. Just like a woman.

Good Luck, and get me a copy of all chapters so I will have material to
go on.

Love from both of us,

PG T

119

Country Club Hotel

445 N. ROSSMORE AVE. • HOLLYWOOD 4, CALIFORNIA • HOLLYWOOD 9-2761

August 2ard, I950

Dear Robbie;

I took the book in its present form tonthe
West Coast editor of Colliers, she told me
that she could not give it a fair reading
in its present for, and to have it all
together, one white and six onion sheet
copies. I have the paper and a public
stenographer standing by when it is ready to
be typed.

The first part of the story where Jim left
homw and returned with the horses is not in
my files. That I want, also the Molin Rouge
episode where he cleaned out the famous
place to protect two American women.

Also get the deal in about him having been i
the merchant Marine during the the last wab

Jim even went to Washington try ing get into
the abmed forces, and finally wound up on an
ammunation ship bound for India. Lets soft pedal the drinking, I had
Warners out it out completely. Ther is plenty of good material with
out using that, especially at the time of the Olympics.

I am not soolding Dear, but I want this booknto be the best ever done
on Jim and to go on forever and ever. I am sure you know what I mean.

It is to be for juvihile comsumption too, and after Jim is dead and
gone, the book will still be salable if the proper treatment is
given. Times awastin darlin, lets get this book ready for sale and
put it over big. Warner Bros are starting their publicity on the
picture next week and that should stimulate great interest with
potential publishers, I shhll be awaiting your book in its final
form. Take time out to do it as we all wish it to be.

Bye for now, if you wish anything in a hurry, call long distance and
reverse charges. The tying alone is going to run into money at this
end. The stenographers have a set price for that sort of thing. See
what price you can get in Philddelphia, if it is cheaper than here,
we will pay for it. Bring Jim out as a great man as well as a great a
athlete.

Bye for this time.

Love from both Jim and

Patricia

Tell people coming this way to stop at this hotel.

MEMBERS: N.S.C.

HILLSIDE 3111

JIM THORPE'S
Thunderbirds
ALL GIRL SOFTBALL CLUB
6161 MELROSE AVE.
HOLLYWOOD 38, CALIF.

August 24th 1950

Dear Robbie;

Please take the time to sit down and read your story. It is very disconnectd and I am not scolding you. If you will start over and run this out as fast s as possible I can sell it.

Have the continuity running smoothly. I do not have time to rewrite and arrange. I am now busy getting ready to open our place.

I should like to have the story back, as quickly as possible for I am to have it typed properly for Colliers. That is going to cost about $25.00 with the copies, but I had rather have it done out here where Jim and I can edit it before the final preparation.

The weather here, is horrible as always, fog and wet morning and night and steaminghot during the day.

I have a lot of hard manual labor ahead of me getting our supper club ready for the opening.

Jim is tied up every day at Warners. He is going to have publicity pictures this morning.

Good luck daer, but concentrate on the book for the time being /x/ or I just cant do anything with it.

                    Love from both of us.

                         Patricia

Country Club Hotel

445 N. ROSSMORE AVE. • HOLLYWOOD 4, CALIFORNIA • HOLLYWOOD 9-2781

• In the heart of Hollywood
• Overlooking the exclusive
  Wilshire Country Club golf course
• Magnificent Swimming Pool
• Sunny Terraces and Landscaped
  Gardens
• Excellent Cuisine
• Smart Cocktail Lounge

445 N. Rossmore Ave. (Vine St.)
Hollywood 4, California

October 5th 1950

Dear Orlo;

I am playing hookey from the club, this
morning to get out some of the correspondenc
which has piled up o n me in the past three
weeks. Jim and I have bean spending every
waking hour out there, and have been working
very hard, long hours, and things are
beginning to look good at last. We had a ful
house last night. Sold out all the steaks
chicken barbequed ribs etc. and I am having t
to hire an assistant for my cook$

DONT EVER BUY A NIGHT CLUB!   It is hard
work plus.

Enclosed is the forewood you asked for.

I have heard nothing from Miss Bilkie at
Olliers, I do not know if that is good or
bad. I have just returned some rough sketches
to Multi Products, of Chicago, who are making up the things on
Jim.

I will try to find a publisher here on the coast to take up
the book, if I can find the time.

I must be out at the club inside of an hour and will bb there
until two A M,

This is the first time in weeks I have sat down to write any
letters and I have a huge stack which I will not have time to
take care of this morning.

I do not feel that I can afford to pay fpr publication now, as
we are putting all our money into the club and trying to build
up a stock for the holi days. Could I have gotten hold of the
story last summer, I could have done it. Now we do not have
the money to spare.

I will do what I can, but I am spreading muself so thin now I
am in a constant state of collapse.

Do you not know any literary agents, in New York, who will sell
the story, and neither of us w ll have to bother with it.

Bye for now. I must run, Affectionately,

Patricia

JIM THORPE
WORLD'S GREATEST ATHLETE
Country Club Hotel
LOS ANGELES, CALIFORNIA
HOllywood 9-2701

December 5th 1950

Dear Orlo;

We have heard nothing from Collier's. I am enclosing a letter which I recieved yesterday which is self explaining.

The induction into the Hall of Fame at Oklahoma City was most impressive and cost us plenty.' I am writing the publisher of the Tulsa World, to learn if he will be interested in running your story in serial form, while we retain all other rights.

While in Oklahoma, I slipped on the ice turned my ankle and am now on crutches, which is a big help when I am loaded down with things to do.

Jim will call, Miss Bilkie, west coast editor for Colliers this morning and try to learn what all the delay is about.

I have not submitted the story to any other person yet, but it do does occur to me that after over three months they would know if they want it or not?

Have you tried to make any other contacts for publication? I wish to heaven I was in the east. Every thing comes out of New York. Anything submitted here still goes to the east coast for approval.

We have sold our place. The work was much too hard for me. All responsibility fell on my weary shoulders and it was just too much. How ever we get a good deal, inasmuch that we recieve a monthly payment plus interest.

If we can get our affairs into shape quickly we will come east. I wish to get Jim's appearances with the picture lined up, the people in Oklahoma want Jim to return there to make his home, but the idea does not appeal to me too much.

I have been given the word that,(Movie agents have gone to work on sports editors?) regarding all publicity regarding Jim Thorpe. Have you had any such information? It seems fantastic that Warners would so stick out their neck, it would be an out and out libel suit if this were true. Will you please advise me if any such information has come your way?

May I hear from you as to your opinion of the enclosed and also if you can dig any information out of Colliers at your end. If the above ban has any foundation it may be possible that Colliers are observing said ban, and if true we can raise

plenty of H... out here. Love from both of us

Patricia

HOTEL Statler Palm Springs BUF Calif

Thursday, A.M.

Dear Robbie:

Arrived ~~in~~ Los Angeles - week ago today - The American Air Lines ruined my typewriter - I have not yet had time to contact them regarding it.

I was frightfully ill for three days after I arrived & had _so_ many things to do

I am sending the books today - Came down here for a desperately needed rest. I'm practically on the verge of a collapse.

6 miles out of the Springs on a date ranch & love it - No noise or commotion only about 6 people know where I am - no telephones etc

Write me Gen-Del Palm Springs Calif.

Good Luck & My best

Patricia

JIM THORPE
WORLD'S GREATEST ATHLETE
Country Club Hotel
LOS ANGELES, CALIFORNIA
HOllywood 9-2701

SUNDAY

DAER ORLO:

I HAVE BEEN TRYING TO GET THIS LETTER OFF TO YOU FOR OVER A WEEK
I HAVE THE MSS. IN THE HANDS OF COLLIRES MAGAZINE. THE WEST COAST
EDITOR HAS SENT IT ON TO NEW YROK.

WE HAVE BEEN WORKING LIKE DOGS TRYING TO GET THE SUPER CLUB WE
BOUGHT HERE, CLEANED UP, DECORATED AND OPEN FOR BUISNESS. WE HOPE
TO HAVE OUR DINING ROOM OPEN THIS WEEK. I DO NOT HAVE A FINGER
NAIL TO CALL MY OWN.

THE TYPING COST ME TWENTY FIVE DOLLARS, AND I FURNISHED THE PAPER.

WILL YOU PLEASE TRY TO CONTACT SOME PUBLISHERS IN NEW YORK I SIMPLY
HAVE NOT HAD THE TIME, AND AM ON THE VERGE OF A COMPLETE COLLAPSE.

THE NIGHT CLUB IS TAKING SIXTEEN HOURS A DAY OF MY TIME AND I COME
HOME SO TIRED AND MISERABLE I CANT SLEEP, HOWEVER, JIM IS DOING
ALL RIGHT AND NOTHING BOTHERS HIM.

I HOPE TO GOD WE GET GOING OUT THERE. WE HAVE POURED MONEY INTO THE
PLACE AND WILL HAVE TO MAKE IT NOW OR GO UNDER. THE LOCATION
PARTY IS BACK FROM OKLAHOMA AND THERE WILL ONLY BE A SHORT TIME
OF SHOOTING LEFT HERE ON THE COAST. MOST OF THE PICTURE ID NOW IN
THE CANS.

PRAY HARD FOR US TO MAKE GOOD, AND PLEASE TRY TO GET TO THE
PUBLISHERS THERE. I AMD GETTING DISHES SILVER AND KITCHEN
EQUIPMENT TOMORROW, AND WILL NOT HAVE A MINUTE FOR ANYTHING BUT
THE CLUB FOR SEVERAL WEEKS, I WISH I COULD HAVE A REST BEFORE WE
OPEN I AMD COMPLETELY WORN OUT.

YOU ARE NEAR AND CAN OPERATE BETTER FROM YOUR END.

LOVE FROM BOTH OF US AND GOOD LUCK.

Patricia G. Thorpe

The encolsed will show you what I had in mind regarding a
syndicated coluṃn for Jim, I should like you to ghost it if you
can and get it through the kings Features or another syndicate in
new york?

MEMBERS: N.S.C.   HILLSIDE 3111

JIM THORPE'S
Thunderbirds
ALL GIRL SOFTBALL CLUB
5162 MELROSE AVE.
HOLLYWOOD 38, CALIF.

Palm Springs Calif
Friday

Dear Robbie;

Your note recieved. I think it would be very nice for Pop to do the fore
word. His address is, Glenn S. (Pop) Warner. He is very gracious and will
co-operate with you.

I am out here at the Springs trying to get some rest. I returned from L A
yesterday, after having a complete physical. I have an ulcer a liver and
kidney condition, and must have a complete rest. I've been trying hard
but the mail and telegrams come through. I have stopped all long distance
calls. I doubt very much if Jim can get away long enough to meet you any
place but Buffalo. This man he is under contract to, is definitely a
stinker. and if I was'nt so sick I would go back there and kick his teeth
out!

I had a lovely letter from Jim Clark today, and I will have to get that deal
through no matter what. He jas really nailed me down now where I must state
my terms. I do like the man though. He is smart besides being a Democrat and
a Catholic. I think Jim will be better off connected with him than any other
person in football.

Make as many connections as you can in publishing. I was supposed to write a
letter to the Dell Publishing of New York and Beverly Hills re;- the cartoon
book Ive been so sick I hav'nt even done that.

So, try to get along without me. Will you please send me a reciept for the
books I sent. I am sure they will be a great help to you. Also send copies
of the chapters you have so far for my approval.

Freeman of Warners is being so sweet I am bewildered. It seems that most of
my fighting days are over. Well I hae to get an ulcer to be in the swim,
All the agents in Hollywood boast one or more!

Good luck dear boy, hop to it and do a story second to no one, Freeman tried
to get me to take you off the book and hire a Hollywood writer. I told him
I had absolute confidence in your ability to turn out the book I wanted, so,
that was that.
I must write to Clark now. Jim has been getting offers from all over the
country, but I still want him with the Eagles.

So bye for now, with the best of good wishes and the best of luck with the
book'

Patricia —

Gallery

Jim and Iva Thorpe

Courtesy of the Oklahoma Historical Society

Jim and Patsy Thorpe

Courtesy of the Oklahoma Historical Society

*Jim Thorpe played for and managed the Oklahoma Indians
baseball team, also known as Harjo's Indians, in 1933*

Carlisle Industrial School welcome home from the 1912 Olympics

Jim Thorpe

Courtesy of Jim Thorpe Memorial Foundation

Jim Thorpe's children;

Jack, Grace, Bill, Gail, Phil, Charolette, Richard

Courtesy of Jim Thorpe Memorial Foundation

Jim Thorpe

Courtesy of Jim Thorpe Memorial Foundation

Jim Thorpe

Courtesy of Jim Thorpe Memorial Foundation

Jim Thorpe

Courtesy of Jim Thorpe Memorial Foundation

Jim Simpson celebrates his 50th year in sports broadcasting January 9, 1993 on ESPN. Pictured below with Simpson in 1948 is Jim Thorpe in the WOIC-TV studio in Washington, DC (currently WUSA).

Jim Thorpe Interview

Courtesy of Anita Thorpe

Jim Thorpe

Courtesy of Jim Thorpe Memorial Foundation

*Walter Battice (Sauk and Fox) (left) and
Jim Thorpe (Sauk and Fox) (right).*

Courtesy of the Oklahoma Historical Society

Courtesy of the Oklahoma Historical Society

Courtesy of the Oklahoma Historical Society

Courtesy of the Oklahoma Historical Society

New York Stadium

Courtesy of the Oklahoma Historical Society

Courtesy of the Oklahoma Historical Society

Courtesy of the Oklahoma Historical Society

Courtesy of the Oklahoma Historical Society

Courtesy of the Oklahoma Historical Society

Carlisle School

Courtesy of the Oklahoma Historical Society

American Indian Olympians

Courtesy of Jeff Payne

Carlisle vs. Springfield

Courtesy of Jeff Payne

1912 Carlisle vs. Springfield

Courtesy of Jeff Payne

1912 Carlisle vs. Springfield

Courtesy of Jeff Payne

www.ingramcontent.com/pod-product-compliance
Lightning Source LLC
Chambersburg PA
CBHW051204120626
46547CB00012B/1195